T0117922

Drunk & Disorderly, Again

Testimonials

Erwin Krasnow - Former general counsel of the National Association of Broadcasters and of counsel with Garvey Schubert Barer. *"Drunk & Disorderly, Again is wonderful bedtime/airplane reading material. I enjoyed reading about your triumphs and setbacks. You have led a fascinating life and have done a good job of telling about how you evolved on life's journey. You are a good writer. The book is entertaining and inspirational. (My enjoyment in reading the book was enhanced by the fact that I know ... or at least heard most of the "characters" that you encountered during your radio days."*

Mindy Frumkes Miami, Florida Radio personality and "Mindy & Malo" show Miami, Florida

"I have never been exposed to the inside life of someone I love and care about who has been plagued and suffered as you have. I never really understood alcoholism at all - your words have given me so much insight. I am aghast and sad at some of the difficult and awful things you have experienced, my friend - and all the more thrilled at how you have and are WINNING by living a wonderful life full of so much love and positive energy."

John "Rio" Carrillo (Mr. Leonard) – aka: John Calhoun for ABC's syndicated morning show - **"Best Country."**

"I just read "Drunk And Disorderly," it's terrific. I can tell it was written from the heart."

Jhani Kaye, Program Director K-Earth 101 FM Radio, Los Angeles.

"My friend and mentor. I'm happy that you're getting recognition for putting something really good out there for others to read.. I want one of the first copies.

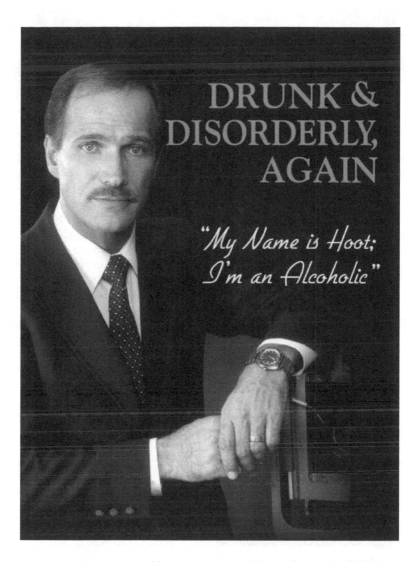

DRUNK &
DISORDERLY,
AGAIN

*"My Name is Hoot;
I'm an Alcoholic"*

CLAUDE "HOOT" HOOTEN

New York

Drunk & Disorderly, Again
My Name Is Hoot, I'm An Alcoholic

Copyright 2009 Claude Hoot Hooten. All rights reserved.

No part of this publication may be reproduced or transmitted in any form or by any means, mechanical or electronic, including photocopying and recording, or by any information storage and retrieval system, without permission in writing from the author or publisher (except by a reviewer, who may quote brief passages and/or short brief video clips in a review.)

Disclaimer: The Publisher and the Author make no representations or warranties with respect to the accuracy or completeness of the contents of this work and specifically disclaim all warranties, including without limitation warranties of fitness for a particular purpose. No warranty may be created or extended by sales or promotional materials. The advice and strategies contained herein may not be suitable for every situation. This work is sold with the understanding that the Publisher is not engaged in rendering legal, accounting, or other professional services. If professional assistance is required, the services of a competent professional person should be sought. Neither the Publisher nor the Author shall be liable for damages arising herefrom. The fact that an organization or website is referred to in this work as a citation and/or a potential source of further information does not mean that the Author or the Publisher endorses the information the organization or website may provide or recommendations it may make. Further, readers should be aware that internet websites listed in this work may have changed or disappeared between when this work was written and when it is read.

ISBN 978-1-60037-548-4

MORGAN · JAMES
THE ENTREPRENEURIAL PUBLISHER

Morgan James Publishing, LLC
1225 Franklin Ave., STE 325
Garden City, NY 11530-1693
Toll Free 800-485-4943
www.MorganJamesPublishing.com

In an effort to support local communities, raise awareness and funds, Morgan James Publishing donates one percent of all book sales for the life of each book to Habitat for Humanity. Get involved today, visit **www.HelpHabitatForHumanity.org**.

I dedicate this book to my extraordinary wife, Sande, who has made me so happy. I didn't know life could be this much fun.

Living with a sober alcoholic can be very challenging because there are things about us that just "ain't quite right."

So thank you, honey, for taking this "one-time bad penny," rubbing off the old oxidation, and giving me a new shine.

Acknowledgments

I would first like to thank my Higher Power (HP), whom I choose to call God, for giving me the courage and words to express myself. I honestly didn't know I had it in me to write *Drunk & Disorderly, Again*. I wouldn't be alive today if it wasn't for God's love and nurturing. There were so many close calls.

To my wife, Sande: thank you for your encouragement, writing skills, patience, love, and strong heart. More than anything though, I want to thank you for accepting the words written on these pages.

I especially thank my Alcoholic Program sponsor, Ernie, for keeping me on course in sobriety. I know it wasn't easy, but I am a drunk, and I have special needs.

David Hancock, Megan Washburn, and the inimitable Rick Frishman, my friends at Morgan/James Publishing, could not have been more helpful and supportive. I thank you for your guidance and mentoring.

Special thanks to Fairy Gilbert, Thomas Brown, Tom Elliott, and Alexis Adkins, whose critiques and editing skills helped me make some sense of *Drunk & Disorderly, Again*.

To my golf partners, Bobby, Butch, and Coach Gilbert: thanks for understanding when I was too busy writing to not play golf, even though it saved you a few bucks in the long run.

With love and gratitude, I'd like to acknowledge the late, wonderful Dr. Wilbert Greenbaum, who opened the door that gave me a second chance at life, and to God and my Alcoholics program for showing me how to live it.

"The worst thing that happens to you can be the best thing for you, if you don't let it get the best of you."

— Will Rogers

Contents

Foreword

"My God!" I called him a *gook* and slurred, "It's too bad we didn't get the rest of you Vietcong sons of bitches while we were at it." I didn't realize he was one of the owners of the nightclub doing business with our radio station.

I was in a blackout, incoherent and unable to stand on my own two feet. No doubt the radio station would fire my ass this time. All I ever wanted was to "be somebody." How did I get here—drunk and disorderly, again?

The nightmares and miscues of my life and career have been so numerous and embarrassing that I can barely bring myself to think about them, much less admit to them. So, read on my friend; maybe you can avoid what happened to me in Houston, at one of that city's most chic nightclubs. As a top radio personality in the market, it was devastating.

I sincerely anticipate you'll read what you need to get your life on track, without having to fail as many times as I did. By the time I got it, forty years had rolled by.

Eventually, I was able to enjoy a wonderful, sober life, but I want that for you right away. You *do not* have to suffer any longer.

The Houston episode was just one example of the life I was living as an alcoholic. The horrors I went through and those I put others through are numerous and sad, but avoidable.

The key to recovery is acceptance and honesty. In *Drunk and Disorderly, Again*, I point out the signs that may help you identify with me, if you have a problem. No one wants to admit they're an alcoholic, since the only accepted treatment is abstinence.

When I first realized I was an alcoholic, I thought to myself, "I'll have to give up the one thing that gives me joy in my life." That sort of thinking is laughable, considering the pain it caused myself and others, and the way I behaved, thinking it was normal for humans to act the way I did.

No matter what you think may happen, once you've been sober for a while, and begun to develop relationships and friendships in sobriety, behaving as a sober individual, you'll know what I've discovered: Life is wonderful and more fun than ever without alcohol waiting in the bushes to sabotage everything you've achieved.

Chapter 1
Alcoholism 101

I was enjoying another great day in paradise, sitting at the Tiki Bar near the pool at the King Kamehameha Hotel on the Big Island of Hawaii. This was the day when I would be given a preview of the rest of my life.

The inventory list of the people, places, and things I'd lost or screwed up as a result of my drinking was getting longer every day. The wreckage of my past was strewn all along the highway of my life.

As usual, I was feeling no pain, drinking and checking out the babes poolside, when in walked this guy I had played golf with that morning at the Kona Country Club.

He was especially memorable because he showed up at the golf course smelling like bourbon. Not that there's anything wrong with that—it's just that it was 7 AM. Hey, I was a drunk with standards! No booze before, oh, I don't know, 9 AM? He wasn't a bad golfer either, for a guy who was *three sheets to the wind* that early in the day.

1

"Hey, Paul, what're you drinking," I queried.

"Jim Beam, straight up," he responded. "How you doing?" I motioned to Kemo, the bartender. Paul looked like he'd had his own battle with booze. I could only imagine his nightmares.

As he sat down next to me, he told Kemo, "If you see my glass half empty, bring me another."

God, he even drank like me—one right after another.

Then Paul smiled and added, "Don't get behind, Kemo."

We laughed.

We drank through the afternoon, telling stories and taking turns buying each other drinks. Paul's face looked like it had worn out a few bodies in his lifetime—very rough.

He picked up the beer he'd switched to and stared at the label for a moment as if to collect his thoughts, then said, pensively, "I've had a love-hate relationship with this shit all my life. I've never been able to get a grip on my drinking. I'll do alright for a while, and then I have to fight my way out of some kind of a nightmare or another. God, I'm sick of it. Kemo, bring me another one."

"I tried AA," he went on, "but that didn't work. I'm married to my fourth wife." He paused for a second, as if to reconsider whether it was worth it to spill his guts to me. Then he continued.

"She more or less leaves me alone. She only cares whether there's enough money to buy what she wants, which is cool by me, so long as she stays off my ass. My kids won't have anything to do with me. My son's been on a five-year bender of his own, and my daughter thinks I'm a loser. You know what, Hoot? She may be right!"

I wondered why Paul was confessing his personal failures to me that afternoon in Hawaii. I knew firsthand the agony of a drunk—the misery and feeling like a failure. I was really getting bummed out, when

I realized that Paul was telling me a story that I could complete if his memory lapsed. He was telling *my story*.

I took a close look at Paul. Even though he smiled a lot, the happiness in his eyes was overruled by the emptiness coming from his heart.

The years of misery showed clearly in his face—a face that looked like it had faked one too many smiles. I listened to his story and saw my future that afternoon on a bar stool in Hawaii.

Chapter 2
How to Get Sober in Forty Short Years

I was at a meeting of alcoholics a short time ago, when a pretty young woman in her early twenties, whom I'd seen many times, turned to me and said, "Can I tell you something? I mean I don't want to say something that might, well...."

She paused. "I'll just say it," she continued. "You are so handsome for an older man. I just hope that I marry someone who looks like you do when he gets to be your age."

Getting older has its advantages, including not having to explain the goofy things I do, like leaving my keys in the fridge or putting a carton of milk in the pantry.

I liked what she said, but at the same time, it was like having the rug jerked out from under me. On the one hand, it meant a lot to me to still look good to someone as young as her, but on the other, it reminded me that time is running out.

I thanked her, but somewhere within me, I realized that the hole wasn't filled. My life was decidedly better. I was sober, and money was no problem anymore, but I realized what it was I was missing. Love! Bone-deep love. I wanted someone I could care about and share my life with. I just wanted someone to kiss my face. I needed someone who wanted to be with me.

Lately, the way the years are flying by is downright scary. Months feel like weeks and years seem like months. I don't like it. Don't get me wrong; it's good to be alive. The senior discounts aren't bad, but man, I'm running out of time.

Living in the present has always been difficult if not impossible for me. I was never happy with the moment I was living. No, my "now" was always tomorrow. Tomorrow showed promise. Tomorrow was hope. It was where my dreams were. Tomorrow would offer me another chance. Tomorrow was where I was a winner, a big success—it was where I was going to be famous.

As the Good Book teaches: You can't change the past, but you can ruin the present by worrying about the future (Matthew 6:34). Very funny, especially because that's an exercise with which I became quite proficient.

I couldn't capture who I was or where I was going early in my life, but I did know that the only thing I was interested in, from the time I was a young boy, was being on the radio.

As a kid, I'd sneak my radio under the covers with me at night and listen to "the world." The big show at 9 PM was "Lucky Lager Dance Time." I fell asleep listening to it, and other shows, almost every night, which probably explains why I need something to listen to as I doze off.

Eventually, I would load up my low *self-esteem* and a giant lack of *self-worth*, sprinkled with a sizable helping of *self-loathing* and ego, to offer my talents to the world of broadcasting.

It's now forty years later, and to paraphrase what talk show host Neil Boortz says, "I was able to take a large order of character defects and turn them into a pretty good living."

I did well on the radio in my hometown of Los Angeles—considering I was only three years into broadcasting when I was recruited—and then I spent some years in El Paso, Texas, mostly having fun, and then it was on to Houston. In Houston, I reached the top and the bottom of success at the same time.

My failure in Houston would lead me back to Mother AA, whose apron I would hide behind, off and on, until I finally found sobriety. Soon, I began to have longer stretches of sobriety and even managed to have the top show in Miami for a number of years. The victory was bittersweet though, because I couldn't stop drinking completely.

Finally, I struck gold in Santa Fe, New Mexico. It's now tomorrow in my life, and I'm ready to review what I have to show for it. Stay tuned.

Chapter 3
History of a Drunk

I come from a long line of overachievers and drunks, dating back to my cousin, the great Sam Houston. The Cherokees in Tennessee, whom he loved as brothers and sisters and married into, called him, "The Raven." They also called him, "The Big Drunk."

Like Sam, I drank to get drunk and I didn't stop until I got there. I didn't know if I was going to be a happy drunk or a horse's ass. I always began in a good mood, especially during the first few beers, which I chugged to feel that initial satisfying high that filled my body with happiness. It wrapped me in warmth and good feelings as it flowed through my veins. That first dose of alcohol that coursed through my body told me, "Everything is going to be all right now."

Once I started, I didn't know if I was going to drive home drunk or pass out at the bar, in my car, or God knows where. Ironically, the "first buzz" was one of the few times when I was living in the moment.

As far as it goes, I would rarely recall any of it, because most of the time, I was in a blackout. You know us; we're the people who can't remember anything the next day. It comes after drinking a lot.

For me, it came sometime after the twelfth or thirteenth beer, followed by a few nods from my old pal, Jose Cuervo, not to mention an occasional trip out to the car to take a couple of hits from my Sweet Mary Jane.

Miller Time was all the time. I can't tell you how often I stood on the corner of Fifth and Vermouth, and slipped into the Last-Ditch Attempt Saloon for another shot of misery. I'm not sure who wrote, said, or sang that—Tom Waits, I think—but the seat at the end of the bar was reserved for me. I sat on it for almost forty years.

I've experienced the highest of highs a man should be allowed to enjoy, but I also lived through the most excruciating, bone-crushing lows that no one should ever have to endure. Somehow—and God only knows how—I lived through it. I continuously kept making the same decisions, while hoping for a different result each time. Now *that* is the definition of insanity, and I am living proof.

My name is Hoot, and I'm an Alcoholic.

Chapter 4
How Young Is Too Young?

No one would have dreamed how that first drink, back when I was just five years old, would alter my life—forever. It was exciting, warming, made me funny, and gave me balls. So while I was growing up, I couldn't wait to be old enough to drink.

Later, at age eleven, I stole a bottle of wine from a grocery store and my pal Larry and I took it down to the river and drank every drop of it. I told Larry that it would make us feel real good. He had never drank before, so we got drunker than skunks. That experience would complicate my future drinking career. I didn't know how to deal with getting so drunk that I lost complete control.

I would spend forty years trying to get a grip on my drinking, but failing miserably. I tried lying to my parents, by saying that Larry and I found the bottle down by the river and only took a few swallows. I'm sure my folks dismissed it as just another one of many behavioral problems that I was having at the time.

It used to be that if you had a drinking problem, when your name came up, someone would simulate drinking with a hand gesture to their mouth, and that would pretty much remove you from the running. These days, unless you've got a rehab rap sheet, you're kind of a wuss. It's almost a prerequisite to fame. Robert Downey Jr. had his problems, and then Tatum O'Neil and Lindsey Lohan as well, just to mention a few. In sports, too, a couple of felony convictions *"Ain't no thang!"*

Back in the day, if you were guilty of any one of these infractions, you could forget about a career. Celebrities were to be looked up to and had better keep it clean. As a boy, one of my first heroes was a pole-vaulter, Bob Richards, who set the Olympic record in that event.

I was a pole-vaulter as well, and I would have been devastated if he had been anything less than the great athlete and man he was. The "Reverend" Bob Richards went on to live up to his reputation with honor.

Chapter 5
In the Beginning

I was born in Los Angeles in the fall of 1941, the last of Jasper and Audrey Hooten's three kids. We lived on Woodlawn Avenue, just south of downtown L.A.

The world was changing fast when I was born, mainly because of World War II. Mom and Dad were building planes for the war effort, and the world was a busy place. It was all about Rosie the riveter, the symbol for the women in factories, while most of our men were putting their lives on the line for freedom and the Red, White, and Blue.

Dad had already served in the army, and even though he wanted to fight, they needed him and thousands of other patriots to build airplanes here at home.

I have a vague memory of flat-bed trucks with planes loaded on them moving down the streets, with traffic pulling over to the side to get out of the way. There was lots of war news on the radio—Walter

Winchell with the latest from the war front, and Edward R. Morrow with his nightly reports: genuine excitement.

These were my early radio heroes. These were chaotic times, but I enjoyed them. As a result, the greater the chaos and turmoil, the clearer and more deliberate I become. Calmness rattles me; it makes me uneasy.

My dad was handsome. He did some modeling in New York in his early 20s, but those were tougher times as it was the middle of the depression, and he couldn't afford to depend on the off-and-on world of modeling. Dad, like his dad and three of his four brothers, was an alcoholic until the day he died.

Everyone called my Dad "Hoot," except Mom. His name was Jasper, but he hated that name—which was something I wished he'd thought about before naming me Claude.

Dad and his four brothers were all raised in Benton, Arkansas by a hard drinking, strict Baptist minister for a father and a mother who would just as soon kick your ass as look at you. I would become acquainted with her wrath soon enough.

My Mom was a tall brunette with a million-dollar smile and sky-blue eyes. Her side of the family had some celebrity, including Timothy Matlack, "The Fighting Quaker" and Continental Congressman. His handwriting was excellent; experts agree that it was he who actually penned the Declaration of Independence.

He was also the scribe who wrote General George Washington's appointment as the Commander in Chief of the Continental Army. Too bad his writing talent wasn't passed on to me. My handwriting looks like the scribbling of a drunken doctor.

After the war ended, we moved out to the San Fernando Valley. Dad got a job delivering milk door to door for Golden State Dairy. He had some famous movie stars on his route; one of them was Harry Morgan, the actor.

Morgan was a big star back then, but he was most famous for a role that would come later in his career on television. He played Colonel Sherman Potter on the show "MASH." Dad said Morgan was a really nice guy, and even gave my pop a five-dollar tip for Christmas that year, which was pretty good money back in the mid-forties.

I had my first brush with the law at the age of four. My brother Brad convinced me that it would be a good idea to take some matches out and set fire to the grass field behind our house. I remember striking the matches, dropping them, and seeing the dry grass catch fire so quickly.

I ran like hell. Brad, who was just two years older than me, tried to stomp the fire out, but couldn't. The neighbors called the fire department; they got there right away and put it out before it caused any real damage. It scared the crap out of me, but the fire trucks were cool.

Brad confessed to our dad that he put me up to it and got a pretty good licking. In the future, I would routinely set fire to grass, but only when it was neatly rolled in a Zig-Zag paper.

Dad, was a tough, no nonsense kind of man. He was in favor of whatever it took to bring peace, law, and order. He'd been an MP for six years in the army. He ruled by force and fear in his house.

Discipline was Dad's friend, but me and mister discipline never got to know each other, at least not well. Good thing I was Dad's favorite. He rarely dropped the hammer on me.

Sadly, my father mentally and verbally abused my sister and downright beat my brother. Dad did not know how to cope with the challenges of parenting, having little or no skills. He was what is referred to as a "functioning alcoholic"—one who survives life, is able to work, and keep some of his ducks in a row, but generally fails in most areas.

The almost unthinkable scenario that prevailed in my family was that Dad, somehow, thought my brother was not his son. Anyone who knew my mother, a loving Christian who was devoted to her family and husband, would know that my father was so off the mark it's almost inexplicable, but as a result, he would beat my brother over almost anything.

Seeing my dad corner my brother and slug him with his fists was devastating, not only for my brother, but my sister and myself as well. My sister would jump in the middle of the fray and curse my father, while our mother would beg him to stop. I would usually cry while it was going on. I was so frightened, and I would plead for Dad to quit. Finally he would, and then he'd pick me up and love me. Talk about mixed emotions.

God, it was a nightmare for a young boy like me. There's little wonder why my brother and sister ended up hating me. Long after my pre-teen sister went to live with my grandmother Russell and my brother joined the navy, they thought my good life with dad continued. They didn't know the horror scene I would eventually live through. So, my brother spent his boyhood trying to please his father, to somehow get dad to love him. It just wasn't going to happen. It was like swimming with a shark. You never knew when he was going to turn on you.

My brother was very angry in his early years, but burned most of it out on the athletic field. He excelled at everything, especially football, where the stadium announcers knew his name and number by heart. Over the stadium speakers you'd hear, "Hooten in on the tackle," over and over again. I had my work cut out for me when it came to living up to his good name on the sporting field.

Later, when my brother came home on leave from the navy after a couple of years in Hawaii, he had begun to mature and had developed hair patterns exactly like our father's. It showed in his chest hair and hairline. Wow! My dad realized how wrong he had been, but was still unable to show my brother his love the right way. He tried to make up for the past, but some things can't be fixed.

Beautifully, my brother fathered two boys and two girls. He was and is a wonderful father; he stopped the cycle of violence in his generation. He, my sister, and myself would not let anger live in our homes.

Back in "The Valley," when I was five years old, we lived next door to a Mexican family. Their oldest boy was my brother's pal, and I went to kindergarten with Rosie, their little girl, who was about my age. She cussed like a sailor. She could rattle off a string of words in a tirade that would make a maestro of four-letter words blush.

One day at school, Rosie taught me a new term, "Asshole." It sounded funny, so, I dared her to use it on one of our classmates. When she did, the boy immediately said, "Teacher, Rosie called me a dirty name."

Rosie got in trouble for it because the teacher actually heard it. I got in trouble too, because she promptly squealed on me for "putting her up to it." Thus began my formal education regarding women.

I got drunk for the first time in my life during the fall of 1947. I was five, soon to be six years old. Occasionally, Dad played host to his brothers for Saturday night poker. As the night wore on and everyone loosened up, they'd let me drink the last swallow from the bottoms of their beer bottles. One Saturday night, I sensed my first pangs of having to have some of that brew.

After topping off the bottom of one more bottle, I began to feel the warm, euphoric, "I can do anything" feeling associated with the first rush of booze as it flows over your taste buds and settles warmly in your stomach.

When my Uncle George wasn't looking, I pulled his bottle of beer down behind the chair and took several deep gulps of it. Very quickly, I could feel the high coming. I staggered and began to giggle.

Dad noticed and said, "Claude, you'd better get to bed or I'll have to call the cops and tell them you're drunk." They all laughed.

I actually thought he might just call the cops, so off I went to nighty-night land with a full-fledged buzz on. Now, it's not that I went on a three-week binge, started a tab at the local dive or anything, but once I opened the door to drinking, it stayed open. Especially since my first experience being drunk brought me attention, laughs, and a warm glow. I wanted more. I liked being shit faced. I couldn't wait to get old enough to drink.

My Uncle Lloyd, a cook at the famous "Pantry" restaurant on South Figueroa, convinced my dad that there were some opportunities in Grants Pass, Oregon. So, with my sixth birthday coming up, we were about to head up the Oregon Trail.

Chapter 6
Over the River and through the Woods

While mom and dad made the move to Grants Pass, Oregon, they sent me to live with my Grandmother Ruth (Hooten) in Levelland, Texas. It was the tumbleweed and dust capitol of the Texas panhandle, if not the world.

The wind was always blowing, and it was unbearably hot in the summer. The afternoon breezes would gust up to forty or fifty miles an hour, mixing sand, dust, and debris into a massive, nasty aggravation. The cars in that part of Texas looked like they had been sand blasted, their coats of paint dulled down to primer and steel.

Grandma Ruth, who would just as soon kick your ass as look at you, had long since left Grandpa Hooten, the Baptist minister. Mom told me many years later what prompted the break-up. One day, the good reverend came home soused and mad, and then took his anger out on her and the boys, again.

Word was that Grandpa got so mad at her that he picked up a hatchet and hit her in the head with it. He didn't hit her hard enough to kill her, but it knocked her out and left her with a nasty scar and an attitude to match.

She was not easy to look at. Her jowls made her face sag so much that it looked like she had a permanent scowl on her face. I don't know why, but she made up her mind that I was going to be a no-account kid, so she rode me like a mule. She backhanded me every time I disagreed with her, right or wrong.

I tried to stand just out of her range, which wasn't easy since her knuckles almost dragged on the ground. I called her the "vanilla gorilla," because that's what I thought she looked like. She didn't walk so much as she waddled, but she could waddle really fast.

After a number of years of her abuse, I went on the offensive and took to screwing with her, hoping not to get caught. I would do anything I could think of to rub her the wrong way.

The best came several summers later when, once again, I was sent to spend a few weeks with Grandma and Grandpa. It was like two weeks of boot camp. She would save up all her backbreaking chores for me so they'd be waiting when I got there.

She'd get my butt up at 5:30 in the morning, serve me a big breakfast, and then it was work, work, and work. It was all part of her I'm-going-to-make-a-man-out-of-this-one plan.

Part of it was cool. The year I was thirteen, much to my delight, Grandma decided that it was time to teach me how to drive.

I was going to be fourteen that fall, and in Texas at the time, you could get a driver's license at that age. So, Grandma took me out to her '49 Ford for a driving lesson.

"You let the clutch out slowly," she instructed. "That way, the gears will take hold and you can accelerate. Then, you push in the clutch again so you can shift into second gear." Just at that moment, I popped the clutch accidentally. The car lurched forward violently as it tried to get enough fuel into the carburetor and grab first gear, finally grinding to a dead stop.

Grandma took her left arm and smashed me in the chest. "That's not what I told you to do," she chided. "You let the clutch out slowly so it won't lurch."

She'd hit me real hard, but I didn't care. I was getting to drive the car. Within a short time, after a few more direct hits to my young arms and chest, I got it down pretty well.

One afternoon, she was on my case about something. (It was always something.) I'd had it with her. So, when she was taking a nap before Grandpa got home, I went out to the driveway, which was on a slight incline, and backed that '49 Ford down so that the back bumper and trunk were sticking out in the street a little. It was not protruding enough to cause an accident, but it was enough for grandpa to accuse her of not setting the emergency brake. She shot me a you-did-this look that made me think she was going to come up off the couch and start beating the truth out of me right there on the spot. She knew I did it, but couldn't prove it. Reasonable doubt was what I was shooting for. I just shrugged my shoulders, pretending not to know a thing about it. She was beet red and really pissed. I was doing double back flips in my head, trying not to laugh out loud, hoping none of the neighbors had seen me do it, knowing there would be an inquisition.

Although I pushed her buttons, she did have power over me. One time I made the mistake of casually saying "shit" in front of her. Oh, my God! She grabbed me by the arm, dragged me into the bathroom, and literally washed my mouth out with soap. For days, everything I ate tasted like Lava soap. When mom came to get me, I was at last released from Grandma Ruth's jail. Get me out of Levelland, Texas. Please!

As we left Levelland, the train we took was loaded with soldiers coming back from the war. They constantly whistled and flirted with my mom, who seemed to enjoy their attention without letting them know for sure. It set off an emotion inside me that I didn't completely recognize until later. When women would come on to me, my self-esteem would soar and my masculinity would be validated. That feeling would prove to be more addictive than any substance I could drink, snort, or smoke.

On the way to Oregon, the train stopped in Santa Fe, New Mexico. At that time, it seemed like a dusty little outpost of the Old Wild West. Who could have known that many years later, I would find tremendous success there, both in business and in relationships.

Chapter 7
The Oregon Trail

G rants Pass was a lush, rich overgrowth of bramble and vines with the Rogue River flowing through the middle of it all. It was a boy's dream.

East of town, up the river, there were rapids that dropped down into a deeper river bed flowing under the railroad bridge, past the park, and under the Caveman Bridge, where traffic crossed the river going north and south. The name "Caveman" had been taken as the motto for the town because of the nearby Oregon Caves. The bridge was comprised of half-circle mounds of concrete; leap-frogging across both sides of the bridge was a thrill and a challenge for us kids.

We boys would race to see who could run over the half-circle humps above the traffic and get to the other side first. I'm lucky to be alive. It was so dangerous, but when you're a kid, it's something you just have to do. Boneheads! I don't know how many times the cops chased us off, threatening to take us home and tell our folks.

Wild flowers grew everywhere in Grants Pass. As I walked home from school, I enjoyed the smell that came from the honeysuckle that hung over the fences. It was an exquisite fragrance. I loved the beauty of the floral palette and the wonderful, fresh aroma that seemed to just hang in the breeze.

Really, it was as if the whole town was one big Glade Plug-in. Every now and then, I'd pick a handful of the different variety of blossoms growing there and take them home to Mom.

It's a special memory for me, because I remember her delight when I'd take the time to bring her flowers. Also, I now know, she saw a softer side of me that she tried to nourish as the years went by. Dad was a man's man. His motto was, "You only do manly stuff."

Blackberries grew wild along the river, which we later learned we could pick and sell to the bakery up on Sixth Street. They'd make delicious blackberry pies and other tasty pastries. It was a great way to earn extra money. Extra, heck, I never had *any* money. It gave me some financial independence, which was nice. Getting a buck out of Dad was nearly impossible.

The railroad bridge that spanned the Rogue River upstream turned out to be the location of a boys' rite of passage. To become a man, all you had to do was jump off the bridge into the river from the trestle level.

At the base of the bridge, on the south side where the main support was, there was a dock ten feet above the river. This turned out to be the town's swimming hole for local boys. No girls allowed!

A heavy cable swing dangled from the base of the bridge. We would swing out from the "Ten," at dock level, or you could take it up to the "sixteen," the more challenging level. We'd grab the cable and it would throw us way up out over the river, where we'd let go in order to do a variety of acrobatics before hitting the water. It was exhilarating—just the kind of cheap thrill I'd spend my life chasing.

Now, as bridge history went, when a boy felt that he was ready to become a man, he'd step up to the edge of the trestle and jump. Too often, though, it would take forever to build up courage, even though everyone was egging him on. More often than not, he'd chicken out.

So, during my time, we devised a foolproof method to assure that this rite of passage would happen in a timely manner. Beneath the trestle were a series of support bars. When a boy thought he was ready, he would climb down under the trestle and grab onto one of the struts and hang there until his fingers just couldn't hold on any longer.

Even if a kid changed his mind, no one was allowed to help him up. Eventually, he'd be too weak to pull himself back up and would have to drop into the river.

I was ten years old when I finally came into my manhood. I had determined not to beg anyone to help me. It seemed so wussy, and anyway, I didn't want the ridicule that came with trying to chicken out.

The moment finally came. My heart was pounding so hard I could see it pulsating in my eyes. Then, as my fingers gradually weakened and I let go of the struts, I instinctively leaned forward to see what was below. I saw the river coming up at me, which was a big mistake.

I was dropping very fast. So fast, in fact, that when I hit the water, the impact knocked the wind out of me and slapped my chest and face a bright shade of pink.

I was overjoyed I had finally done it! I didn't let on that I could barely catch my breath when I first emerged from the water. That first jump scared the daylights out of me, but by the time I swam to shore, all my buddies were cheering me on.

It took another two weeks before I did it again. I stood at trestle level and jumped, stiffening straight as I hit the water, cutting through the river like a knife. I loved that thrill. It was exciting, and after all, I was a man now! All that really paid off later when I was a swimmer and diver of some note in high school and later in the Air Force.

In those days, Larry Powell was my best friend. We did everything together. I met Larry in the first grade and we stayed tight for many years. Larry and I built just about every conceivable floating contraption that two boys could. After all, we lived on a river.

The most fun we had was with logging-truck inner tubes. We were well known down at the tire shop. They'd let us have and repair those old tubes. We'd fix 'em up and roll 'em down the street to the river, neither of us more than half the height of those big tubes.

We'd take them way upstream and then float two or three miles downstream. Not too far from where we ended up on our tubes stood the tower of a radio station. It was on the south side of the Rogue River, called KUIN.

Coincidentally, one of the personalities at the station was the father of one of my classmates'. I was excited the first time they let Larry and me in to take a look. It was thrilling. From then on, I pestered them constantly to let me watch. I wanted to be on the radio. I wanted to be somebody. In my mind, being on the radio would get me there.

I was in the fourth grade with the boy whose father was a newsman on the radio. I quizzed him constantly about his father and the radio station. We were in Mrs. Grosh's class. She fed my other passion—to travel and see the world.

Mrs. Grosh encouraged me to send away for tourism and government brochures from the countries I was interested in. My first packet came from the *Republica del Ecuador*. Mrs. Grosh was very excited for me, and told me about a train that went from the coast, way up into the Highlands of the Andes.

Years later, I would experience the thrill of enjoying that great little country, Ecuador, and leave with several hundred sucres that I won at one of their casinos. Mrs. Grosh would've been proud.

That summer was pretty much like all the others in Grants Pass: up early in the morning with my buddy Larry, fishing the backwaters of the Rogue River for bluegill, and then swimming and jumping off the bridge all day. It was great fun!

That same summer I entered the "Oregon Junior Olympics" and won a lot of Gold, Silver, and Bronze medals for sprinting, hurdles, pole vaulting, high jumping, even capturing a bronze medal in the shot put. It was a prestigious event though because later my brother would try to impress a young girl he had the hots for by giving her my medals, telling her that he had won them, the peckerwood.

Everything was about to change. The summer I turned ten would very quickly go from Heaven's innocence, to Hell's horror as my life would move in a harsh new direction.

Chapter 8
Hell on Earth

Every year the carnival would come to town, and we'd help them set up and get free ride passes for our effort. Another buddy of mine, Bobby, and I went out to the fair grounds to see who needed help.

I got a job with the guy who ran a "kiddies" ride—little fishes that move in a circle and up and down like the Merry-Go-Round. I remember how beautiful the weather was: sunny skies, warm temperatures, and a pocket full of free passes.

Wow, I could hardly wait for the gates to open the next day. As we were getting close to finishing, the man I was working for asked me where everyone went to swim.

"Down at the park on the Rogue River," I told him. "There's a platform we all swim out to. It's a lot of fun," I said enthusiastically.

He told me that he liked to swim too but wasn't very good. He was kind of bashful because of it and would rather go to a quieter place.

He had an old pick-up that he let me steer on the way out to "a smaller swimming hole," a few miles from town. He pulled over just before we got to the river in an area of heavy trees and brush. He got out and came over to my side as I was pulling my pants down over my swimming suit, which I always had on.

He grabbed me and said, "Let's swim naked!"

I sensed something horrible was about to happen.

"I don't want to swim without my suit," I yelled.

He was pulling my pants off; I was screaming and crying, fighting him all the way, when he hit me as hard as he could in the side of my face with his closed fist.

I saw stars and felt like I was going to pass out. The fear I felt at that moment was immeasurable! He was still holding me in a vicelike grip, pulling my pants and swimsuit down, holding me close to him as I continued to scream. He jammed his penis into me; the pain was so excruciating that I screamed a shrill, bloody-murder shriek!

It was the kind of scream that you might hear from an animal that knows it's almost dead. Nothing had ever come out of me like that. He was trying to get a better grip on me when I came up with the force to break free and escape, just inches away from his last grasp that came so close to dooming me.

I ran to a safe distance from him, holding my clothes. He wasn't able to chase me because his pants were down around his ankles. He said he was sorry and wouldn't try that again.

"Come over here," he said.

I was weeping and pulling my suit and pants back up, keeping a safe distance from the son of a bitch, as he continued to try to convince me he wouldn't do it again. I was scared to death and was afraid he might do more than what he had already done. I absolutely thought he might kill me.

It was the first time in my ten years of living that I ever sensed that my life was in jeopardy. I kept my distance from him, knowing I could outrun the bastard, as he continued to try to convince me to get in the truck. He said he'd let me steer the truck on the drive back as long as I didn't tell anybody.

I was keenly aware of the risk, but we were miles away from town, or any civilization for that matter, so I slowly moved back toward the truck.

I felt the disadvantage of trying to outsmart an adult, but I pretended to accept the offer of steering as though that was a fair trade for the attack.

All the way back, I kept my right hand on the doorknob, ready to leap in a second. My mind was racing, and my instincts were on high alert. Thank God he kept his word, and when we got back, I was afraid to tell anybody.

I was so ashamed. I didn't tell anyone anything for a couple of days, but when my friend Bobby told me that the same guy had attacked him too, I said I was going to tell my parents.

As I told the story to my mom and dad, my mother was shocked and very angry with the creep who molested me. My dad didn't say a word; he just listened. Mom called the sheriff, who was a neighbor living one street behind our house.

Then, Bobby came over with his mother, and we explained to the sheriff what had happened to us. The sheriff put law enforcement into action, and he sent a deputy out to the carnival to arrest the creep!

As the deputy drove the patrol car back into our driveway, Bobby and I tensed up, knowing that we would have to make a positive identification while he was handcuffed in the back of the patrol car. The pervert's name was, ironically, Jimmy Friendly. I hated him so much that if I had had a gun in my hand, I would have shot him dead on the spot. The psychological ramifications of what happened that day down by the river still haunt me to this day.

There was a time in my mid-twenties when I actually gave serious thought to hunting him down and killing him for all the grief he'd brought me. My feelings are somewhat restrained today, but I have a real problem with pedophiles. Most think that what they're doing to children is okay. It's a sickness that has no cure; a creature defect that seemingly has no solution.

I don't know why, but for some reason they let Friendly go, and my mother encouraged me to just block it out of my memory and pretend it never happened.

I had always been Dad's favorite child, his little man. He would teasingly sing songs about me, constantly ribbing me about everything, especially girls he knew I didn't like. He'd make up playful little silly tunes about me and wear out the old ones like, "Claude and Roberta were sitting in a tree, k-i-s-s-i-n-g!"

In spite of his other side, my dad had a wonderful sense of humor—a side only I would be privileged to enjoy. My brother wanted his love and got none, while my sister hated him outright. Now, it was over for me as well. I was not his little man anymore. Things had changed, and Dad was distant.

Shortly after that awful day, I did something that didn't meet with dad's approval, and he called me a "Queer!" Then I knew. I was smart enough to know what he was talking about, and I was heartbroken. I had wanted my father to kick the shit out of the bastard, to tell me, "It's okay, Son. We love you. It's not your fault."

"I couldn't help it," I explained, sobbing. "He grabbed me and did that to me."

Dad turned his back and walked away as I wept. He walked away for the rest of my life, never giving me anything close to love from that moment until the day he died. I never felt so alone. I just wanted to die.

I had lost my dad forever. Overnight, I changed from being a great kid—athletic, good grades, and a Cub Scout—to a boy looking for trouble. I was heartbroken, completely lost, feeling dispossessed and so unloved.

Suddenly, life wasn't so enjoyable anymore. I cried almost every night. I would have cut off my arm to get my father's love back. I was no longer his son. I guess he thought I could have prevented it. I don't know what he was thinking, but my life would never be the same.

Almost at once, I went looking for trouble. It was obviously my cry for help. I overheard Mom and Dad talking about me one night when I was supposed to be asleep. Mom was saying she couldn't figure out what was wrong with me. *"Hello?"* I thought. "I was just beaten and raped, and my father called me a queer because of it! Gee, I wonder what was wrong."

The early 1950s were very different times than the years we're living now. I doubt my dad even knew what a pedophile was. No one had figured out how to deal with those kinds of social piranhas.

"Maybe we ought to send him to Grandma Ruth's for a couple of weeks," Dad said. Mother agreed. I was doomed. Again.

So, I was sent to Grandma Ruth's in Texas for a few weeks of cruelty to add to my misery. I hated that Godforsaken bitch. I was full of rage from head to toe. I thought, whatever she has, "Bring it on; I'm going to shove it up your ass!"

I was defiant and completely uncooperative. This would not be a battle I would win, however. While I was there, I wrote to my buddy Bobby, bragging about some of the items we had stolen from stores in Grants Pass.

Big mistake. Naturally, Grandmother Ruth opened and read my mail and sent it to Dad. When I got home, Mr. Law and Order was waiting for me. Dad took me to the police station where I was arrested—another milestone in father and son relationships.

I was brought before a judge who threatened reform school at Woodburn, Oregon, which was an infamous boy's reformatory in the state. It worked. I never stole anything again. Instead, it taught me that I needed to be a survivor. However I was dealing with my life at the time wasn't working. Going to jail sounded awful and scary.

The distance between my father and me could not have been wider. Dad made me go to the stores where I had stolen items and apologize for what I had done, and then offer to work it off. I did. I worked hard and was offered a summer job at the hardware store where I had taken a few items. In reality, Dad may have saved my life with that discipline. I really wasn't a thief; it was a cry of desperation.

I guess I got the attention I was looking for, but I felt so alone. My sister was living with my mom's mother in Texas, in that same dusty hellhole that the Vanilla Gorilla called home. My brother spent most of his days and nights living with another family in Oregon. He couldn't stand anymore of Dad's beatings. I felt completely abandoned.

I knew I needed to reload and reinvent myself so I could become independent of anyone who had power over me. Nobody was ever going to hurt me again.

I hated everything and everyone at that point. So, when Mom and Dad tired of Oregon and wanted to move back to Los Angeles, I was ready for what would become the first of many geographic moves that I hoped would bring me some newfound happiness. My childhood had come to a sad and dishonorable end.

Chapter 9
Back to Los Angeles

We moved to Montebello, a very nice suburb of Los Angeles east of "The City of Angels." After a few months living with my Uncle George's family, the only male member of my family who was not an alcoholic, we moved a few blocks away in the same apartment complex.

I had matured in book learnin', so after a few weeks in the eighth grade, they bumped me up to the ninth grade. Darn, I missed having to study square roots. Oh well!

In my neighborhood, I met Dick Edlund. Dick was a year older than me, but we shared a number of mutual interests. During the summers, we'd hitchhike down to the beach, usually Long Beach, because it was a straight shot down Atlantic Blvd. Once there, we'd surf all day and wrap things up with a few rides on the old "Cyclone Racer" roller coaster at the Pike.

We also had photography in common. We built a darkroom together and got into it pretty intensely. Dick had an extraordinary gift for the abstract. We were only thirteen and fourteen years old, but Dick was light-years ahead of almost everyone when setting up a shot. He would manipulate the scenery to get an interesting view, or he'd get a big sheet of cardboard and punch holes of varying sizes and shapes in it and let the light source flow through it, casting an unusual pattern on whatever he was trying to illuminate.

Later, he would receive several Oscars at the Academy Awards for his special effects work on movies like *Raiders of the Lost Ark, Star Wars, The Empire Strikes Back, Alien, and Ghostbusters,* to name a few.

Dick and I were invited to join a Hearst Corporation program for gifted young photographers and journalists. It was called the Scholastic Sports Association or SSA and was sponsored by Hearst and the *Los Angeles Herald-Examiner*.

My life was back on track again. We would take the bus from Montebello to downtown Los Angeles, and then walk over to Eleventh Street, where the *Examiner* was located. Ralph Alexander, an old, battle-hardened reporter who tried to retire but couldn't stay away from the place, was put in charge of us kids in SSA.

He wore an old time fedora that had all the essence of the '30s and '40s, except he didn't have a press card slipped into the felt band. Ralph had been told to quit smoking. God knows for what reason, but his teeth were as yellow as corn. Word was he used to smoke three packs a day, but now he was chewing ten or fifteen sticks of gum at a time.

Ralph was a gruff old codger. He was a combination of Perry White and Lou Grant, but without the people skills. Our job was to photograph highlights of high school athletic events and write the accompanying stories, which were then published in the Saturday and or Sunday *Herald Examiner*.

We would work alongside the professional reporters and photographers at the paper. Most were very nice to us kids, recognizing that one day some of us might be on staff with them. We were a group of talented young folks, even if we were only fourteen and fifteen years old.

That summer was exciting, having the opportunity to work at the *Examiner* alongside the best photographers and journalists in the business. We had time to do what teenage boys do too though. Like when Dick's father foolishly decided he'd get his son a car just to work on. The foolish part was telling Dick, "Now son, you can't drive this car on the street. You don't have a license and it's not safe anyway."

The car was in rough shape. It was a '36 Chevrolet with suicide doors, the interior ripped out, and no door panels or windows, but she ran pretty well. Mr. Edlund paid twenty-five bucks for it.

Naturally, when Dick's dad was at work and his mom was shopping, or whatever, we went roddin'. In Montebello, there was a hill that ran down the backside of town to Pomona Blvd.

Wilson Hill was pretty steep, but dangerous because it was a dirt road that had potholes and loose chunks of dirt lying in the road. We'd take that old Chevy up to the top of the hill and drive her down it. The foot brake was almost nonexistent, so while Dick drove, one of us, usually me, would work the emergency brake, in hopes of stopping that crate before we came up to a very busy Pomona Blvd. at the bottom of the hill.

It was pretty scary, because the floorboards had rotted out, almost completely, so you could see the ground whizzing by. When we'd hit a pothole, dirt would fly up into the cab, and the emergency brake wasn't really dependable either. That didn't stop us from seeking the thrill though.

One day, with Dick behind the wheel, myself riding shotgun and handling the emergency brake, and Gary Anderson and Dave Picket in the back seat, we set out for another Mount Wilson adventure. Dick powered it up too much, and we were flying down the hill, pretty sure we weren't going to stop in time for Pomona Blvd., so Pickett threw open the door and bailed out at about thirty miles an hour, rolling down the hill in a tumbling dust cloud, but surviving nevertheless. There were a bunch of bushes just before Pomona Blvd. that Dick opted to mow down in order to stop.

Phew, it worked. Ha ha. We bolted out of the old car and the dust poured out with us, but no one was hurt. We rolled it over to the gas station close by and pooled our resources to put about forty cents in the tank to get back home. I think it bought us a couple of gallons of gas though. That's why they're called the good old days.

The rest of that summer was a little more subdued, as Dick and I both spent our time surfing, taking photographs, and working in our darkroom. Later that fall, we worked for the *Montebello Oiler*, our high-school newspaper, and we were the star students in the photography class. I was a sophomore, and Dick was a junior in 1956. Sophomores were not allowed to take photography as an elective, but because of my elite status with the *Los Angeles Herald-Examiner*, I was given the privilege of participating in the class.

The teacher loved our work, and encouraged us to share our knowledge with the others and help them with their assignments.

Chapter 10
Drunk and Disorderly, Part 1

The Montebello High School Oilers were playing El Monte High School in football one fall evening. Dick and I were assigned to shoot the game for *The Oiler*. Prior to the game, Dick, who looked older than I did, was able to buy a couple of quarts of Thunderbird wine down at the little Korean store in "Jim town."

"Jim town" was a kind of Mexican barrio in south Montebello. We discovered that the little Korean lady there at the market couldn't tell how old we were, or pretended not to, so that became our booze connection.

We didn't intend to drink all the wine that night, if you want to call it wine. I thought it tasted like shit, but the dizzier we got, the more we laughed, and the more we drank, the less we could taste.

We drove up to the game in El Monte and pulled into the back of the parking lot and polished off the wine. It was awful, but it got us where we wanted to go and beyond.

While photographing the action of a football game, the idea is to stand on the sideline about ten yards down field from where you hope the play will develop, so that you can shoot the action when it comes into your zone. We had both taken a few good shots when we thought it would be a good idea to run along with the play, shooting the action as we did.

With all the coordination of two developmentally challenged Orangutans, we were stumbling and falling all over ourselves. We got the crowd's attention too, and they were laughing their butts off at us.

Oh, God! Mr. Ody, the Dean of Boys, who was about fifty feet away from us, motioned for us to come over to him. Ody, as we called him, was not amused with what he was seeing. He was short and bald and didn't put up with any crap. We were screwed, no doubt.

Ody had a look on his face that I had never seen before. He grabbed me by the arm and said, "You boys been drinking?"

It was more of a statement than a question.

"No sssssssir, we haben't been drinkin'." I slurred. I could hardly speak I was so drunk.

It was even more difficult to explain to our parents, who were called to come pick us up. So, I was right back on Dad's shit list, again. It was just one more reason for him to keep his back turned on me.

We were both suspended from school for three days, and to make an example of us, they kicked us out of our beloved photography and journalism classes. I was embarrassed beyond description. I was glad when the suspension came, just so I wouldn't have to face my classmates.

That really stung. Our entire lives had been wrapped up in photography and journalism. That also marked the beginning of my begging for one more chance. It didn't work then, but as time wore on, I was able to hone my contrition skills to a fine degree.

I'd show them. In my junior and senior years, I screwed off, taking only the classes I was required to take. I chose life guarding for three periods a day, and then I was on the Water Polo, swimming, and diving teams over the school year, filling out my PE requirement. By the way, I won every single diving competition as a senior. Still, I missed photography and journalism. I harbored a major resentment toward the school and began to experience almost uncontrollable rage.

We lived in an apartment complex just off the famous Whittier Blvd. in Montebello. Families occupied most of the units, so there were lots of kids in the neighborhood. Right behind our place lived an absolutely gorgeous girl named Kathy. Kathy was about fourteen and I was going to be sixteen pretty soon, so I was beginning to notice things. I wasn't just lookin' now; I was *lookin'*.

Kathy was beautiful. She was the sexiest girl I had ever seen. She had a naturally beautiful baby face, but was built to drive men crazy. We had seen each other many times, but the last few times I wanted to say something to her, and I could tell she wouldn't mind.

One day as we passed each other in the complex, we both stopped and began chatting. We liked each other instantly. She had light-brown hair, blue eyes, and was a very curvy 5'4" or so. She truly could have been a centerfold for Playboy.

It was about three o'clock in the afternoon, and she had slipped into some very sexy shorts after coming back from the beach. Honestly, I don't know what happened, but I knew that my folks wouldn't be home from work for another hour or so, and the next thing I knew, we were tearing the clothes off of each other in my bedroom.

Wow! It was my first time ever, and I was shaking in anticipation. We kissed and kissed, but I was scared to take it the rest of the way until she lay back in my bed and pulled me down on her. I had never known anything like this. It didn't last long, though. What did I know about endurance? I was a sprinter.

Thus began a new and sometimes fanatical chapter of my life, the genuine confirmation of my manhood. She and I would sneak off every chance we got that summer. In the fall, Kathy moved to West Covina, about fifteen miles east, almost cross-country for a kid without a car, but we'll always have Montebello.

I really liked photographing nighttime football. In an effort to show their support of my photographic talents, my folks bought me a very nice 4x5 Speed Graphic Press Camera, with the latest in strobe lighting and accompanying accessories. Mother was insistent that I be given the equipment to succeed. Dad pretty much looked at it as flushing money down the toilet.

A new brain, wiped clean, might have been a better choice, but not an option. So, as a junior, *The Oiler allowed* me to cover games for them. On October 18, 1957, I was the photographer on a cool autumn night, a great night for football.

It was a home game and I felt invigorated. Mom had just bought me a nice, tan suede jacket. I had my hair looking pretty cool, with just the right amount of pomade, a bit of a ducktail, and a few strands of hair dropping down onto my forehead. I was Fabian with a press camera, a good-looking kid of sixteen, as of the week before, and still a bit bashful.

As I moved along the sidelines catching the action with my camera, the Oilerettes, which was the girl's Drill Team, was behind me. Each time the play moved me in front of the girls, I could hear them giggling. They would "woo hoo" me, and stare me down, laughing and pointing.

I was a little embarrassed, but I dug it. I just didn't want to let them know. I mean these girls were the crème de la crème of high school beauties. So, the next time I was positioned in front of them,

I turned very quickly and hit them with the strobe light from my camera. They all jumped. As I was laughing with them, my eyes locked on the prettiest of them all. She was Arlene Morrissey, one of the most popular girls in school. When her eyes refocused, she fixed on me too. She was beautiful, with light blonde hair and blue eyes. All American and all right. She had a smile that took me down. I felt almost helpless. It was the first time I had ever felt that way.

No one had ever hypnotized me like Arlene did right then. Well, Kathy had, in a different way, but it all happened so quickly. I finally broke free from Arlene's gaze and went back to taking pictures. Later, she cooed, "Are you going to the dance?"

There was a dance in the gym right after each game. It was just like "Happy Days." I met her there and we danced and got acquainted. We were both good dancers, and really hit it off.

I stole a kiss before the night was over, and our high school romance was on. She was beautiful, older by a year, a senior, and a straight "A" student. *Pretty good,* I thought. *A step up in class.* Good stuff for an egomaniac with an inferiority complex.

Chapter 11

Welcome to the

Wide World of Drinking

Somehow, I was able to convince a few bars that I was older than I looked. These were ugly, dangerous dives down Whittier Blvd., in East Los Angeles that would look the other way when I ordered a beer. It was dangerous in that area. My Mexican brothers didn't take to "patties" moving around on their turf. Like a lot of drunks, I liked to drink in the shit holes. It's called "drinking with lower companions." Sometimes, it was difficult for me to determine who the lower companions were—me, or them.

I was a pretty good pool player, but I discovered that if you played too well, they'd think you were hustling, and it could get your butt kicked. I don't know what it was that drew me to these dives. I did know that when I drank, it made me feel good.

I always told myself I could quit if I wanted, but I didn't want to. No, sir! When I started drinking, I was drinking, and nothing else. I couldn't do anything else, or at least I couldn't figure out how to.

I was beginning to notch a lot of barmaids on my six-shooter, which was one of my primary purposes for drinking in the first place. If there wasn't a good-looking barmaid or cocktail waitress on the job, then I moved on.

I enjoyed pretty women, maybe too much. I used the excuse that it was okay for me to screw around while I was going with Arlene, because she was saving "it" for marriage. Resentments were building inside me—major. To me, it was like the ultimate rejection. I got even by chasing everything in a skirt.

After going with Arlene for almost four years, she never told me she loved me. Like her virginity, she was saving the "L" word for the right moment. Now I know this may sound crazy, but on top of loving Arlene, I hated her for what she was doing to me. I knew I should have broken up with her, for her and for me, but I was too immature. I clung to her desperately, as she was my only connection to the sane world.

While I was in high school and for a few years after, I worked for Finley's Color Lab in Montebello, processing amateur film.

I earned enough money those years to pay my own way, as Dad put it. Bill Finley, the owner, took a liking to me. He knew that my dad and I had a rocky relationship, even though he didn't know why. Mr. Finley took me under his wing and treated me like his own son.

The first company Christmas party at Mr. Finley's house just after I graduated from high school didn't go well for me. I got drunk—really drunk. I can't remember much about it, but I was given an accounting of my behavior later—a debriefing I got used to over the years, shortly after checking my car out for whiskey dents.

We black out drinkers can't always account for what we do when we're drinking and driving, so sometimes there is a dent or two we can't explain. Ah, the perils of driving drunk. I can only thank God that I didn't kill someone over the years driving in a black out.

Anyway, at Mr. Finley's party, I got blitzed and sequestered myself in a coat closet, making a scene and not coming out. Finally, after some coaxing, I unenthusiastically came out. One of the first recollections that came back to me from that blackout was remembering Melanie, our receptionist at the lab, coming into the closet and giving me a kiss, a big one, plus a couple of exploratory "feels."

For a while afterward, I thought it was a dream, but it was a blackout flashback. Now, there's no technical term for that, but after a period of time, certain scenes within blackouts open up in your memory. It can actually be horrifying. For years, and every now and then today, I still recall something I don't want to remember.

Melanie was engaged to be married. She never brought it up, and neither did I, but I knew, and I think that she knew that I knew. She just wanted a little. Nevertheless, I was in a blackout, but this time it was different. I snapped out of it on the way home.

One of the little old ladies who worked at the film lab gave me a ride. Halfway there, I came out of the blackout. I was lucid, coherent, and curious. I asked her what had happened.

"You got drunk and went a little crazy," she told me.

I was embarrassed and befuddled. How could I sober up, just like that? I nearly quit my job at Finley's I was so humiliated.

Blackout drinkers, like me, live in constant fear, wondering if we did something horrible, or embarrassing, the night before. When I first began drinking regularly, at around fifteen years old, I thought my blackout behavior was typical for anyone who drank, thinking that it was what alcohol did to everyone. When I discovered that I was an exception in my group, I began, unsuccessfully, trying to curb my drinking just enough to keep from going into the other dimension, known as a blacking out. Raising the bar on drunkenness—how can you top that?

I wouldn't find the escape route out of a blackout for many years, until I discovered the rejuvenating power of cocaine. It happened quite by accident. Flashing forward for a moment, Ariel, one of my drinking buddies, and I had been bar hoping in Miami, Florida when we popped into a dive in South Miami to meet his coke dealer. I was just about gone, and almost in a black out.

As Ariel went straight into the men's room to score, I staggered up to the bar and asked for a beer. I slurred a little and wasn't too stable on my feet as I walked up to the bar stool. The bartender looked me over really carefully. I sensed that he was going to cut me off, but he wasn't sure about my condition.

He reluctantly brought me the mug of beer I ordered, and while he was busy elsewhere, Ariel stuck his head out of the bathroom and motioned for me to get over there. He had a couple of hits of cocaine waiting for me, which I promptly snorted, practically inhaling the spoon and anything else he had in his hand.

I noticed instantly that my balance returned, the slur in my voice was gone, and my thinking was back on straight. When we went back to the bar, I struck up a cordial conversation with the barkeeper, which I could tell had him puzzled. I sounded sober as a judge—new technology.

There's a revealing study, conducted by Alcoholics Anonymous that discusses this aspect of drinking. It's a look into the alcoholic's behavior that says, for the most part: Admitting to being an alcoholic is the last thing any of us wants to do. No one wants to think that he is mentally and physically different from his fellow man. So it should come as no surprise that our drunk-a-logs are riddled with many failures with our drinking, trying to prove we could drink like a normal person. Most alcoholics believe that one day they'll be able to get a grip on their drinking and be able to mix with most drinkers on the same level. This kind of thinking can be characterized as one of the key obsessions of most abnormal drinkers. Many alcoholics chase this belief to their death.

Pretty scary, huh? If a person is in denial of his or her drinking problem, it's easy to say, "Thank God I'm not that bad." For me, there was no denying the fact that I had a major drinking problem, yet I still held out for an easier, softer way.

I wanted someone to slap me on the wrist and say, "Now slow down a little, don't drink so much." I wanted one more chance to control my drinking. "The next time will be different," I'd say. Almost always, the next time was just as dreadful, if not worse than the time before.

Alcoholism is a progressive disease. If you put the plug in the jug and don't drink another drop for ten years, and then go out drinking, your disease will have progressed by ten years. It's as if you didn't stop at all. That's a fact. I would find out eventually, that the only way to begin true recovery was to let go absolutely.

Admitting that we're powerless and incapable of doing anything about our alcoholism and that we're unable to manage our lives is the first step to recovery. (This is not where the preaching begins, by the way. This book is purely the story of how I clawed my way out of hell. You might relate to some of what I'm saying and get something out of it, but I won't be preaching.)

It took me many years before I would fully let go of my old self. In the beginning, when I listened to alcoholic horror stories, I'd think, "Those are extreme cases. That's not me! Don't compare me to that. I'm unique. I'm different. If you had lived through some of the same nightmares I did, you'd drink too."

Another characteristic of alcoholism is immaturity. Our minds don't mature the same as non-drinkers. Alcoholics generally experience an extended adolescence. When I first earned six months of sobriety, I couldn't believe the maturation process that took place in my head in that short period of time.

My second chance at sobriety was really the fiftieth. When I first read *Powerless Over Alcohol*, I thought, "Well, I'm not completely powerless," and "I'm handling things okay, so I can't say, 'My life is unmanageable.' I mean, I'm working and paying the bills."

This when I had already been through two wives, lost all my friends, been thrown in jail a couple of times, lost a few jobs because of my poor performance, and lied about everything, to myself and everyone else.

I have a T-shirt one of my friends in my alcoholics program gave me that says, "I'm probably lying." It's hilarious to most of us on the program, because all of us recognize that it is one of the key symptoms of alcoholism and we've all lived through it. It's funny now, but it was awful when we were living it.

Chapter 12
Small-Market Radio

Arlene and I married a month after I turned twenty. Deep down, I knew I was committing Arlene to a world of misery, but I thought, "Screw it. Maybe things will change." I was hoping our marriage would help me settle down, and allow me to get a grip on my drinking.

I was hopeful that the responsibility would encourage me to mature and settle in as a happily married man. I truly thought I'd been born with a wilder-than-normal side, and that I'd grow out of it.

Early in our marriage, I studied journalism and broadcasting at night, while working during the day delivering furniture for Sears.

My daughter Cindi was born in January of 1964. My childhood Doctor, James Reames, delivered her. Dr. Reames was an extraordinary man. He was Greg "Pappy" Boynton's flight surgeon, from the real "Baa Baa Black Sheep Squadron" during WWII.

He delivered my beautiful little blonde-haired, blue-eyed angel. I felt a new love in my life for the first time—a kind of love I couldn't explain. It was all new, this love, and it was strong and powerful. I immediately felt a phenomenal affection toward her. It came from deep within, as if it had been buried deep inside, but wouldn't come out until the exact right moment. Cindi's birth was that moment.

I studied for a time at Los Angeles City College in Hollywood, trying to determine my major. Only three fit my requirements for creative expression, freedom to travel, and avoidance of any actual labor: journalism, photography and broadcasting.

Finally, Don McCall, the professor of telecommunications, encouraged me to pursue the career I had always wanted: radio. Being a broadcaster, in a way, was a pipe dream, even though I dreamed of it all my young life.

McCall had himself been a big-time announcer for the old Don Lee-Mutual Broadcasting Network. It was primarily a west coast operation that owned KFRC in San Francisco and KHJ in Los Angeles.

McCall was a friendly but serious man with a beautiful voice. I felt like a little kid when I was talking with him, his voice was so baritone. He was tall, maybe 6'1", very skinny, and he looked and sounded like John Carradine, the actor. His brown hair was combed back like Howard Hughes from an era gone by.

His low, resonant voice would almost make things in the room vibrate. After the first semester, he took me aside and told me that I would likely be one of a couple of people in his class that had a chance to succeed.

He said the odds for success were small, but that I had a better than average chance to make it. He advised me to read everything I could get my hands on, so that no matter what came up, I'd at least know a little about it.

1965 brought a new and exciting Top 40 radio format to Los Angeles, called "Boss Radio." It was Bill Drake's clutter-free, smooth, fast-talking, one-hit-after-another idea.

Drake created ideas like "20/20 News" and counter programming, by "sweeping music across the top of the hour," while his competitors aired news headlines. After turning around the fortunes of Fresno's KYNO-AM, Drake applied similar tactics to take KGB from worst to first in San Diego, and then on to KHJ in L.A.

KHJ quickly jumped from no one listening to the number one radio station in Los Angeles. Boss Radio was here to stay. KFWB Channel 98 and 1110 KRLA would soon be knocked off.

I wanted to be on a Boss Radio station, but I wanted to do more than read flip cards. Within a few months, I landed my first gig at a little radio station in Thousand Oaks, California. KNJO (the voice of the Conejo Valley) was co-owned by a local dentist and baseball great Sandy Kofax—who, by the way, led the Los Angeles Dodger's to a World Series win over the Minnesota Twins that year.

The station, 92.7 KNJO, was located in a shopping center on Thousand Oaks Blvd. The whole station didn't take up more than 300 square feet, if that. I was kind of bummed that it was only an FM station, but it was a radio station. At that time, AM radio still ruled the radio waves.

Not too many people had FM in their cars or homes then, and even fewer were equipped to receive stereo. What's more, fewer FM stations were set up to deliver in stereo, but KNJO was in Stereo Multiplex. It sounded phenomenal.

Bill Sommers, the general manager, was only twenty-six years old himself, but he was educated and very polished, and had a surprising knowledge of radio sales and radio in general. He also did weekend's on the air at KACY radio in Port Hueneme, the hottest rocker in Ventura County.

Bill would later move on to be one of the top executives at ABC/Cap Cities, running their Los Angeles operations. He was a great guy and we stayed in touch for several years. Sommers talked me into selling radio commercials in addition to my on-air duties.

I was a natural at it. I loved radio so much, and believed that we had the power to draw people in to buy merchandise. Besides, advertisers seemed to like me. Being on the air was still my top priority, however. I wanted to be somebody.

I had another friend at KACY who told me the name Claude Hooten had to go. Over beers one night, Johnny Daren and I came up with Brad Edwards as a new air name for me. It was a combination of mine and my brother's middle names.

While at KNJO, I met my first radio groupie. Between 6:00 and 7:00 PM, and during my marathon from noon to midnight, I was the host of an hour called "Stereo by Starlight." During that hour, I would feature semi-classical music and a lighter commercial load.

One evening the phone rang, and a sexy voice on the other end admonished me for mispronouncing a composer's name. I told her that I was new and not too familiar with the classics and that I would watch it from now on.

She laughed a sultry laugh and asked me where I was from. I told her Los Angeles, adding, "More importantly, where are you from?" She told me that she was an artist and that she spent a lot of time on the French Riviera. "What kind of accent is that?" I queried. She said it was a combination of a variety of accents as a result of living in so many different countries, as her father was a writer. "Wow," I thought. "What is someone like this doing talking to a bad coin like me?" That's the beauty of being an alcoholic; it's always there to remind you that you're not worth a shit.

I continued to quiz her, not wanting to seem too anxious, but dying to find out what she looked like. "Do you look like your accent?" I asked.

"What do you mean by that?" she wondered. I told her that my mind was racing with images to go with her voice, but that I couldn't tell if she was dark and sultry or blond and lively. She said she had dark hair that "Comes right down to my, my, well you know...."

"Your ass?" I blurted out like a bonehead.

"Well, yes," she replied. "And my eyes are green, and I'm about five foot five."

"Perfect," I thought.

"You sound like Raquel Welch," I said hopefully.

"Pretty close," she replied.

Wow! I couldn't believe it. I get to be a star *and* partake of a beauty buffet as well. Oh God, I love radio.

This was way before people started lying about what they look like in online chat rooms. In between records, I worked on her for a couple of hours, but it wasn't until just before midnight that I was able to finally talk her into letting me come by for a quick hello. Yeah! Sure! A quick hello.

She said her name was Victoria. She lived in a very posh section of Thousand Oaks. Thousand Oaks was nice to begin with, but her house was like a hacienda on the side of a hill. It was a beautiful home. Oddly, she had asked me to come to her bedroom window, which could be dangerous. I could be shot as a prowler or Peeping Tom, but a hard-on knows no danger. In spite of the extra dark night, I found the window and the candle she said would be burning on the sill. I reluctantly eased up to the window and whispered her name.

"I'm here," she replied. "I'm glad you came."

That same sexy, hypnotic voice, dancing on the waves of scented candle smoke, came wafting out. I couldn't make out what she looked like. It was so dark that if it hadn't been for her sultry voice coming out of the window, I wouldn't have believed that there was anyone on the other side. She was like a reluctant cat; the closer I came to get a look, the more she backed up into the room.

The entire situation was very bizarre, and was a testament to the lengths I'd go to try and satisfy the emptiness deep within me. That damned unfulfilled "hole" again.

She served me a beer—one of those really small beers in cans about as big as your thumb. I drank about five of them before I pulled the ruse of the evening. Knowing that a lady wouldn't want me to take a leak out in the flower bed, I said, "Victoria, you've got to let me in so I can pee."

There was panic in her voice. I knew that something was amiss, but I just couldn't put my finger on it. I thought that maybe she had a really ugly face or was missing a leg or something, but finally she said, "Okay, I'll let you in the side door. Just inside to your right is a small bathroom."

As I came in the side door, my eyes had become accustomed to the dark and I could see the outline of a person in front of me, about five feet away. Instinctively, I felt the wall to my right and there was a switch, which I threw on. It was almost blinding. There in front of me stood Victoria, all four hundred pounds of her. Oh, God! I didn't know whether to bolt or go blind.

Here I was, suddenly thrust into the movie *Shallow Hal*, but without Tony Robbins to hypnotize me. She was startled when the light came on. It was like the searchlights at a Hollywood premiere. She must have seen the disappointment on my face, because she began to cry.

"I just wanted a friend, and I was afraid you wouldn't like me I'm so fat," she sobbed. Her beautiful euro accent was completely gone.

Man, I felt bad for her. I walked up to her and held her face up to my chest and told her that I was her friend and not to cry. I stayed and had a few more beers even though I would rather have chugged a pint of Jose Cuervo Gold.

Outside, as I eased myself behind the wheel of my car I thought, "From now on, if they sound good, I'll add one hundred and fifty pounds."

Chapter 13
Is My Microphone On?

I needed to speed up my early radio career. The money was awful. I had made really good money delivering furniture for Sears. Now, in my chosen career, I was earning chump change. My marriage to Arlene had deteriorated to the point where I would leave for weeks at a time, only to return to the warm, forgiving, enabling arms of my poor wife. Not having much money didn't help either. I was hocking everything, including Arlene's engagement ring, which was a full carat diamond, for two hundred dollars. Pathetic.

I knew that I needed to move up the radio ladder quickly in order to get to a large enough market to make some serious money, so I dragged Arlene and Cindi to Palmdale, California for my first Top 40 gig.

I got the job because I told Bob Mitchell, the GM, that I wanted to sell commercials for the station and do weekends on the air. I got hip to the fact that the sooner you say that sales is your reason for wanting to work for a radio station, the sooner you get hired.

Mitchell wasn't too keen on me wanting to divide my attention between sales and on air. He knew that I wanted to be on the air more than I wanted to sell radio spots, and he was right. The only way I could make that happen was to convince him to hire me and that I'd be able to sell a lot of spots (commercials).

Mitchell gave me the "third" account list, which is the crap list of merchants that nobody wanted to sell or couldn't sell. I took the list and went out and sold my tail off. Mitchell was blown away.

He was a stern-looking man, partly because one of his eyes was glass. Keith Allgood, our program director, described him as having one glass eye and one real eye, and said that, "The glass eye was the one with just a touch of human kindness." The fact was, Mitchell was one hell of a guy, and a very good radioman.

After about four months in Palmdale, I felt I'd polished my air sound enough to move on, but I needed to get a higher grade of FCC License. Mitchell tried to talk me out of leaving, saying that the real money was in sales, but I wouldn't hear it. I wanted to be somebody.

In order to obtain an FCC First Class license, I was required to take a six-week course at Bill Ogden's Radio Engineering School in Burbank, California. I had to make one more stop prior to taking the time off for the school so that I could save up for the tuition and expenses.

I took a job at KREO in Indio, California to do the afternoon show. Arlene and I saved every nickel. Arlene and Cindi stayed with her mom and dad in Riverside for the summer while I headed for the hottest city in California.

The teenyboppers screamed when they met The KREO Good Guys at events and remotes. In an effort to keep my living expenses down so that I could afford the Bill Ogden Engineering School, I roomed with a couple of the bachelor DJs at KREO, Danny Mac and Russ O. I had worked with Russ in Palmdale and recommended him for the job to

"Smiling" Jack Howard, our program director. Russ went on to work in San Bernardino and then in Los Angeles.

We were three decent-looking guys with good voices and a ton of young girls who were wild about us. How can you beat that? With no shame, I dove right into that bevy of unbelievable debauchery.

Musically, the summer and fall of 1966 was most unforgettable for Top 40 radio. The Rolling Stones were hot with "Paint it Black," The Lovin' Spoonful had one hit after another, and The Association scored with "Cherish" and "Gloria." Wow!

Plus, The Beatles were cooking with "Paperback Writer," and who could forget, "My Baby Does the Hanky Panky," by Tommy James and the Shondells? The Monkee's kicked off their careers with "Last Train to Clarkesville," and then there was the Syndicate of Sound's "Hey Little Girl," and "Wild Thing" by the Troggs was on top of the charts. It was a summer and fall to remember.

Danny smoked a lot of dope, but when he would take a hit and then hold the joint out to me and say, "'ear," I would always say "no," and that was even *before* Nancy Reagan began encouraging us all to "Just say no!"

Chapter 14
"Ear!"

It was a hot summer night in August in Indio. All the nights in Indio were hot—really hot. Our apartment was right off the pool, with date trees waving in the warm breeze—actually, make that a hot breeze. Indio was just a few miles from Palm Springs where we did most of our playing. I was just hanging out at the place with Danny and Russ.

Danny fired up a joint and took a couple of hits, and then offered it to me. Like I always did, I said, "Naw, thanks, I don't want any of that shit." Hey, I was a self-righteous drunk; you weren't gonna catch me smoking dope.

"Come on, man, just a little to take the edge off," Danny said.

I don't know why, but I said, "Okay."

I took a hit and held it in.

"Take a couple of more or you won't feel it," Danny instructed.

I just kept hitting on that damned joint until they practically had to pry it out of my fingers. Oh, man. I was so stoned. My mind was racing from one thing to another.

"Oh, God. I've got to get out of here. No. No. Wait. I'll tough it out here. No, I'll go swimming. That's not smart. I might drown. Shit, you guys, why didn't you tell me to stop?"

I was "tripping" and they were laughing at me. How could they be laughing while I'm dying? Somewhere in the midst of my dilemma, we all determined that more beer was the way to our Saturday night salvation.

I thought it was a good idea because I just had to get the hell out of there before I went crazy behind that demon dope. I was about to faint from the fear of how far the dope would take me when Danny said, "You drive. I'm too stoned."

And I did drive.

I carefully pulled out of the parking space from our apartment, which, by the way, seemed to take twenty minutes. KREO was blaring on the radio.

Beau, who would later become famous in his own right, was our weekend guy. Small-town radio includes some oddities of programming. For instance, we also carried Dodger Baseball. It's all about turning a profit, and there's nothing wrong with that.

Danny and I, our eyes redder than a road map of Puerto Rico, were wheeling down the boulevard listening to Beau make the transition from music to the baseball game. The segue from music to the baseball game was done by playing an instrumental record timed out to end at exactly 7:33 PM, which was when the game began.

Beau had missed the back time by about five seconds, which is the radio equivalent of eternity, and he had left his mic on to boot. Danny and I looked at each other as the radio station went to dead air, and then Beau screamed out over the air, "Oh Shit!"

At that exact moment, the Dodger baseball game began with Jerry Doggit saying, "Hello, everybody. Dodger baseball is on the air."

I had to pull over we were laughing so hard. We couldn't stop. My cheeks were cramping. We drove over to the radio station and found Beau in a dead panic.

"Did you hear that?" he blurted out nervously. "God, the FCC is going to throw my ass in jail. Some little old lady already called. What should I do?"

We could hardly stop laughing long enough to tell him not to sweat it.

"Nothing will come of it," We told him. I hadn't laughed that hard in years. It was very therapeutic.

Thus began my "medicinal" thirty-year friendship with marijuana. Pot, Weed, Panama Red, Maui Waui, Colombian Gold, Thai Sticks, Hash, Herbs, and Shit: I smoked it all, but nothing compared to a mind-blowing Lebanese joint slipped to me in Paris, or the mellow innocence of a Costa Rican joint that looked like it was rolled in toilet paper. That joint was so potent; it actually stopped time for a while.

However, we now return to the hot sands of Indio!

Chapter 15
They Said It Couldn't Be Done

I was beginning to sound pretty good on the radio. So I sent a tape of my show to Al Anthony, the program director at KFXM, the number one Top 40 station in San Bernardino and Riverside. To my astonishment, I was offered a job, afternoon drive time too. Now that's what I'm talking about. Being somebody was just around the corner!

KFXM was the number one radio station in San Bernardino and Riverside. It was a large market. I couldn't believe it. Al Anthony said he liked the way I sounded. Wow, this was really big time. I called Arlene, and soon, she, Cindi, and I would be reunited.

"This time," I thought, "I'm going to change. I'm going to work hard, limit my drinking, and quit screwing around with other women. This time, I'm going to be somebody."

San Bernardino/Riverside was the first market where the radio station I worked for was completely dominant in the area. I was about to turn twenty-five. What a fabulous birthday present for me, getting hired at KFXM.

After just over a year in radio, I was already at the highly regarded KXFM 590. You could hear the station for one hundred miles in any direction, and even farther at night, when the signal bounced off the upper atmosphere, which is called a skip.

I was headed for my new job, driving down the interstate going west from Indio and a little past Palm Springs, listening to the Four Tops sing "Reach Out and I'll be There," the Left Bank's "Walk Away Rene," "Kind of a Drag" by the Buckingham's, on the "Famous 59."

"Man, I'm cookin' now," I thought. "Play that '59th Street Bridge Song' by Harper's Bizarre one more time."

It was October 1966 and I was filled with excitement and dreams. This was an enormous step for my career. I was determined to make Arlene happy, and I felt that this would be a good jumping off point.

Al Anthony asked me if I'd like to do the all-night show for a couple of hours in order to work the kinks out before starting the afternoon show. I liked the idea, so I came on the air at midnight, pretending to be the custodian because, as I explained: "The DJ, Charlie Walters, took off and couldn't be found." I had a ball screwing around as the janitor/disc jockey. The phones were ringing off the hook with people telling me that I was doing a pretty good job for a janitor.

I did the show using my "home boy" accent, mimicking my boyhood buddies in East Los Angeles. I called myself Louie, pretending that I just came into the studio to clean up, but found that the DJ was missing.

In later years, I would fill in for Wolfman Jack several times as Louie. Aw, but I was excited being at KFXM. Then came the call that rendered me helpless again. A sweet sounding voice on the other end said, "You're not fooling me. I can hear a beautiful voice under all that goofiness."

Man, she sounded good. I added fifty pounds and it still didn't matter. Remembering Victoria from Thousand Oaks, I experienced a slight mental wince, but I was getting bold by this time and I was ready to take some chances.

She said that her name was Donna and that she was a cocktail waitress at The Zone—a topless bar out on Baseline drive in San Bernardino. She had my attention. As she described herself, it sounded too good to be true. I still had some doubts, but then she said, "Why don't I mix a few drinks, put on something more than the radio, and meet you at my front door?"

I almost dropped the phone.

As I nervously knocked on Donna's door, I could smell her hypnotizing perfume wafting under the door. I was hopeful. She opened the door. Even though the lights were low, I could see through her sheer pink negligee by the candlelight. She was a fantastic looking woman.

She was tall, with brown hair flowing over her shoulders and breasts that looked as though they were fighting gravity for all they had. Her face was beautiful. Whew! Working in San Bernardino was going to be a pleasure. "So much for turning over a new leaf," I thought. Complete betrayal.

Arlene took me back all right, but this time she wasn't so sure it was a good idea. She wanted me to do something about my drinking. She wanted fewer words and a little more action. She was growing weary of my overnight disappearances.

I was a complete jackass, and I knew it. The urgency of needing female confirmation was like a disease of its own. I wanted to change, but there was a driving single-mindedness pushing me to constantly reaffirm my manliness.

Each new conquest, for a lack of a better word, seemed to endorse my standing in the male community. I didn't know how to stop chasing women. It was exciting and fulfilling, but I needed to do something about it because I didn't want to mess up my radio career now that I was on the fast track to fame. Hey, I was on my way to being somebody.

I heard there was a pill you could take that would keep you from drinking, so Arlene and I saw a Doctor in Riverside to ask him about it. Sure enough, it was called Antabuse.

The Doc explained that it was a very serious drug, because once you took it, if you drank, "The alcohol will make you very sick, and could even kill you."

"I don't know about that," I told him. "That kind of scares me."

He explained that the drug, known medically as Disulfiram, changes the way your body breaks down alcohol. If you drink alcohol while you are taking disulfiram, you will experience uncomfortable symptoms, including severe nausea, vomiting, and headache. These symptoms discourage you from drinking alcohol by making it unpleasant.

Antabuse stays in the bloodstream for up to two weeks after the last dose. So, you can't drink on a whim. Moreover, if you're planning on drinking, you have to wait for up to two weeks.

Let me just say this: If you think you're an alcoholic, research this drug thoroughly before you take it. It didn't remove my cravings, and it just frustrated me, because I didn't have alcohol to help me fill the hole and help me make decisions, as lame as they may have been.

A prime example of how desperate a drunk I was, after a couple of months of sobriety on the Antabuse, with Arlene supervising my daily dose, I wanted to get drunk. So, for about a week, I slipped the pill under my tongue and fooled Arlene into thinking I was taking them.

Then, along came the real test. I was emceeing at the Gasser in Riverside. It was a nightclub that had turned the old gas company building into a hot spot. The club was alive; it had a great band, and for me, the beer was free.

I was nervous about taking that first drink since I hadn't cleared the two weeks recommended since my last dose of Antabuse, keeping in mind it could kill me if I drank. My attention was being diverted though; the waitress's were hot. Every one of them had been hired specifically for their looks. The joint was jumpin', and I wanted a drink.

I asked for a beer and took a sip, just to test the waters. Nothing happened, so I took another sip and waited. Nothing, so I took that as the okay, and chugged about half of it down, waited a few seconds, and then polished off the rest of it.

It was time to introduce myself, make a few announcements, and introduce the band. All went well. We were off. All of a sudden, I felt like someone was choking me. I could hardly breathe; it was as if someone's hands were around my throat.

My face was very hot and I felt shaky. My eyes felt like they were going to pop out of my head. I didn't want anyone to know what I'd done, so I slipped into the bathroom to have a look. Holy crap! My face was beet red, and it looked like I had a big splotchy birthmark coming up from my neck and covering half my face. Oh man, suddenly I felt like I might pass out. I could hear the doctor's words in my head: "It could even kill you."

"I just need to maintain," I thought nervously, so I went back into the club and sat down for a minute away from everyone.

My condition seemed to stabilize after about twenty minutes, so I asked one of those pretty little barmaids for another beer. She looked at me and started to say something. Before she could, I said, "I think it's the aftershave lotion. It's no big thing."

I remember her, but can't say for sure which of the other fine-looking barmaids crossed my path that night. Even though the alcohol's reaction to the Antabuse continued, I drank in spite of it. The manager came over and thanked me. He didn't say anything about my face, so it must not have been noticeable in the darkness of the "Gasser."

Shortly, after chugging several more mugs of beer, I would be in a semi-blackout. That's the fuzzy semi-consciousness that I fell into just before I slipped off into the other world that I've mentioned.

Many people function in a blackout and no one ever knows that they are in one. That is a state of consciousness that I morphed into frequently.

The Gasser went down two levels, where the gas company offices used to be. Now, they housed the club's office and a bunch of empty rooms. One of the rooms had a bed in it where the manager would catch a few winks. The next thing I knew, I was in there with one of the barmaids. It was pitch black. I didn't know who she was. I was screwing one of the waitress's though, no doubt. It seemed right at the time, but I disappeared back into my blackout.

The next morning, or afternoon for all I knew, I had forgotten all about the night before and didn't even remember that I had been at the Gasser. I panicked. "Good God, where am I?" I wondered. "I can't see. Wait, I was at the Gasser last night, and I drank a lot. Oh shit, the Antabuse. God, am I blind from the medicine? Wait, I can see faint light close by."

It was the next day all right, and I was on a bed two or three floors down. But what the hell was going on? It was pitch black. I yelled out, "Hello." There was no answer. I fumbled to get my clothes on, and found the door to the room. The last thing I remembered was I was getting it on with one of the barmaids.

I couldn't recollect how we got in this odd bedroom, but as I felt my way out into the hallway, I could hear music above me. Then, about thirty feet away, a faint light was splashing on a piece of one wall.

By the time I felt my way back up to the club, I didn't recognize anyone and no one saw me as I slipped out the front door and almost went blind again, from the brightness of the outside light.

I had practically killed myself with the Antabuse, stayed out all night, and screwed a barmaid. I knew that I would be facing some serious consequences from Arlene, and rightfully so.

I had to be on the air at 3:00 PM, so I hustled home. Arlene was at work at the Mission Inn, and I hit the airwaves right on time, left with the question of whom I had banged in the basement of The Gasser last night.

Chapter 16
Drunks, Sex, and Rock and Roll

"I'm your puppet" was a refrain from James and Bobby Purify and a record that will always remind me of my early days on KFXM. The Rolling Stones "Let's Spend the Night Together" is another one. Especially since when the Stones went on the Ed Sullivan Show that year, Ed made them change the lyrics to read, "Let's Spend Some Time Together."

In San Francisco, radioman Tom Donahue was making waves with a new "Alternative Rock" format. "Big Daddy" Donahue was a pioneering rock and roll disc jockey. Donahue wrote an article for Rolling Stone back in 1967 titled, "AM Radio Is Dead and its Rotting Corpse Is Stinking Up the Airwaves." It was a great time to be in radio.

I was very popular in the "Inland Empire" as the San Bernardino/ Riverside market was known. I had a thirty-eight in the ratings, compared to my competition's twelve. Each day was an incredible adventure. Our mascot was a Tiger, so we were also known as Tiger Radio.

We had a weekly four-page magazine that we published as well. I guess these days it would be called a blog. It included pictures of the DJs and our interactions with listeners and recording artists and other promotional stuff. I was in charge of it for a while, so naturally, the first edition after I was hired was all about me, including pictures. (I was also humble.)

I kept in touch with Donna, the vixen I met my first night on the air. She called me while I was on the air one afternoon and wanted me to come by her place that evening.

"Be ready for anything," she cautioned. "Oh, and bring a friend."

Wow! Okay.

"I'll bring a friend," I replied.

I showed up with one of Al Anthony's pals, Ron, and told him, "It's probably going to get wild, so just be aware." He said he was up for it.

Donna answered the door wearing little more than black panties and a smile which she planted on me immediately, claiming me outright, which made me feel good. I introduced Ron as she stepped back and invited us in. There in the lowly lit living room were two other scantily clad beauties and a guy. He was Alan, the owner of the Zone, the nightclub where Donna worked. I also recognized the little Japanese girl sitting next to him as well. She was one of the star performers at the club. Her name was Seiko, and she did a strip tease that left most men stepping on their tongues.

The other scantily clad body was that of Adele. Adele was endowed with unbelievably large breasts. They were almost freakish. She had forty-four Ds or more, and that's why she worked at the Zone. People came from miles around to take a look at her famous "twins."

"Brad, I just wanted to throw you a little thank-you party for all you've done for us on the air to make the club such a success," Al said. Ron was standing nearby, looking like a deer caught in the headlights.

Seiko had stripped him bare and he looked uncomfortable, in an expectant sort of way. I felt a bit jealous, wanting to get my hands on the little Asian nymph myself.

It was my first orgy, and it couldn't have been more erotic; these were gorgeous women. My marriage, my daughter, none of it seemed to matter. The things that were important to me were booze, drugs, and sex. Oh yeah, and my radio career.

Each of these women was extraordinary in their own way. Nothing decipherable was said for a while, and then Donna broke the silence by quietly lighting a joint.

After a hit or two, she handed it to me saying, "'Ear,"

"My war cry," I thought.

We all smoked and laughed away another thirty minutes, or three hours. I can't remember which came first. Donna had some good grass.

Driving home that night was difficult for me because I was beginning to feel despair over the fact that I seemingly had no conscience. What moral compass? I didn't want any and it didn't matter. Right or wrong, it was all about satisfying me. If Arlene did to me what I was doing to her, I'd be gone. What to do? Amazingly, I didn't have an answer. I'm heading home, expecting Arlene to be there, making our house warm for our daughter and me. It doesn't add up.

The first couple of years came and went quickly at Tiger Radio. KFXM had me as visible as possible, capitalizing on my popularity. I was everywhere. If it was going on in the Inland Empire, I was there.

By the summer of '68 I was getting restless and wanted to move on. Jose Feliciano was singing "Light My Fire," Canned Heat had "On the Road Again," Hugh Masekela scored with "Grazing in the Grass," and The Door's "Hello, I Love You" were all atop the charts.

Chapter 17
It's Good to Be Back Home

Dick Lyons, who had been the evening DJ on KFXM, got a job in Los Angeles at KGBS. He told me he was going to put a good word in for me. Then came the call. It was Charlie O'Donnell, calling for Ron Erwin, the program director at KGBS. Charlie said he had an air shift he thought I might be interested in, but it was only the all-night show. He liked my tape and wanted me to come in to talk.

Charlie had been my hero when he was a big star DJ on KRLA, the "Land of Eleven Ten," in the early '60s. Charlie, Ted Quillan, Dick Biondi, Bob Eubanks, and the famous Kasy Kasem were all there. It was cool being on the phone chatting with him like an equal—big time. I finally felt like somebody.

Charlie would become a big shot at KCOP Channel 13 in Los Angeles. Soon, he struck gold and became the announcer on "Wheel of Fortune." Charlie was a great guy. He wanted me to know he had personally chosen me even though he was leaving. He told me I could start on January seventh.

Starting pay, in 1969, was around $25,000 a year, and went to $32,000 when the new American Federation of Television and Radio Artists (AFTRA) contract kicked in. Wow! I was only making $950 a month at KFXM so I was in tall cotton now.

Even as the all-night guy, I made a lot of money compared to what I had been earning, and I was in Los Angeles radio now. It was nice. Arlene, Cindi, and I moved to Santa Monica where we could see the beach. Life was good.

This time would be different. I would slow way down on my drinking, stop fooling around, and hone my skills in Los Angeles radio. I think I meant it.

In the spring of 1969, KGBS hired Roger Christian to be our program director. Roger had been one of the top DJs at KFWB, the Top 40 powerhouse that I listened to in high school.

Roger was even more famous for his song writing. He wrote a number of hits including "Little Deuce Coupe" and "Don't Worry Baby" for the Beach Boys, and "Little Old Lady from Pasadena," and "Dead Man's Curve" for Jan and Dean. He penned a lot of songs.

Roger came with a great reputation for programming. He and I hit it off right away. What a fascinating guy. He and his wife and kids lived in an exclusive home up on Mulholland Drive. His view was a panorama of the entire San Fernando Valley from the bay windows in the back, and Hollywood from the front. It was breathtaking.

Roger had made some serious money writing songs. You couldn't help thinking about that when you saw the beauty of his home, and the '53 and '54 Corvettes, and the two Cobra's parked in his driveway. He was into fast cars.

The day he invited me to come up and take a look at his place, he gave me a king-size felt bedspread that he said Mick Jagger of the Rolling Stones gave him. Cool! I didn't check it for stains. God knows what kind of DNA could have been flushed out of that thing.

They finally got the line-up squared away by hiring Bobby Dale, a famous character DJ from San Francisco. Bobby was bald as an eagle with just a circle of hair around his ears.

What little hair Bobby did have looked like it didn't have much of a chance. In the back, he let it grow. So when he put on his headphones, he was a study in varying degrees of hipness, or grandpas gone wild. It was hard to tell by listening to him whether he was extremely clever or just ripped beyond repair. He was soft spoken, but had a distinctive, semi-gravelly voice that commanded your attention. He sounded a bit like Wolfman Jack if he was whispering.

Bobby sat down and slipped his Koss Pro 4A headphones over his bald head just as his first record ran out. Five seconds of dead air later, he said, "Sorry I'm late," letting a pause of a few more seconds roll by before adding, "If it wasn't for that light at Third and Western, it would already be tomorrow." Perfect! Why didn't I think of that?

"Spirit in the Sky" by Norman Greenbaum and "Love Grows Where Rosemary Goes" by Edison Lighthouse was ringing in our ears. Man, I felt privileged to be a part of it all.

After I got off the all-night show each morning, "The Emperor," Bob Hudson, would take me under his wing and teach me stuff, like the tricks of improvisation and so on.

He said I could be his "producer," which meant that I would be his Highness's royal gopher for a few hours. I didn't mind. He was a great radio personality and gifted man. The Emperor took a liking to me and told me he thought I'd be a big hit on the radio one day, so he spent countless hours teaching me tricks that would pay dividends many times over the years.

He was extraordinary. His timing and sense for comedy and content was second to none. He would sit at the control board reading the paper with his record running out. Without missing a beat, he'd pop his microphone on and begin a hilarious diatribe on something he had been reading in the paper.

Another thing the Emperor liked to do was play golf. He would drag my tired butt out to the Pomona National Golf Course to play at least once a week. The pro there was a big fan of ours. He let us play golf for free.

Hudson would repay him in spades when he recorded a smash comedy album there in the banquet room. The station teamed Emperor Hudson with Ron Landry from WBZ in Boston and the two of them really clicked.

Bringing in Landry made it possible for me to go home earlier and finally get some sleep. It was not good for the Emperor though, as he now was being enabled. He knew that if he was hung over, Landry would be there to do the show. It was the beginning of the end.

Hudson and Landry were best known nationally for their Grammy nominated vignette "Ajax Liquor Store" (1971), and for having written and recorded four gold albums. The first, "Hanging In There," was recorded at the Pomona National Golf Course and I was there.

We had a crazy operation at KGBS. I was in the company of four Los Angeles on-air legends: Emperor Hudson, Ron Landry, Bill Balance, and Roger Christian. Then there was Dick Lyons, "Magic" Christian, and I as the first-round draft choices of the new guard. Magic was doing a lot of drugs and Emperor Hudson and I did the drinking.

The Emperor was a great guy, but like me, he drank himself into more trouble than he could back out of. Hudson was in his mid to late forties and I was in my late twenties. I only hoped that one day I could be half as good as the great Emperor Bob Hudson.

Chapter 18
Anyone Out There?

I discovered that doing an all-night show on a radio station can be very eerie, especially in a large market like Los Angeles. Plus, it was the late '60s—the days of hippies, anarchy, dissent, the Manson Family, drugs, and, for many, bizarre thinking. There were some odd creatures listening.

Of course, there were hard-working folks stocking the shelves in supermarkets and warehouses. Many folks were traveling through Los Angeles on their way to somewhere. Occasionally, I would hear from an odd individual who called me from a Mortuary in The Valley. He was actually a nice guy, but he seemed to enjoy explaining what happens at a mortuary in the middle of the night. It gave me the creeps. Knowing that our building had once been a mortuary didn't help either.

Also, there were a lot of lonely ladies listening who focused on my every word. Then there was the all-night DJ club. I'm not sure who came up with the idea, but a group of us all-night DJs in Los Angeles would meet at a different bar that would open up at six AM once in a while. We'd shoot the breeze and trade stories about our listeners. It was amazing how many of the same girls we had in common.

It was fun getting together like that. After the third or fourth time, we met at a real dark dive on Vermont Avenue, just north of the Hollywood freeway by Los Angeles City College. My friend Jhani Kaye from KUTE 102 was there, along with Steve Sands from KKDJ and Johnny Williams from Boss Radio KHJ. We were all getting whacked pretty fast.

Sands was smitten with this babe at the bar who seemed more interested in the bartender than anything else. She was the only woman in the bar that morning and she looked suspiciously like a hooker. It didn't take long before Steve had snatched her away from the bartender and talked her into a booth in that incredibly dark bar. We weren't paying too much attention. Steve was a real good-looking guy and had told us he was going to get into her pants.

Sands, whose real name was Sandoz, didn't look Latino; he had golden hair, and big brown, almost bright, eyes. His skin was naturally tan. He was an impressive, handsome man.

When Steve took that tall, hooker-looking babe off into the corner booth, we were betting on whether he would try to go for it right there in the booth, when all of a sudden he stood up and yelled, "What the hell, you're a guy? You son of a bitch!"

He stormed over to the bar where we were sitting, laughing our butts off, as the transvestite beat a hasty departure. I think that was the last all-night DJ club meeting. We knew we'd never be able to top that.

Chapter 19
I'm Almost Somebody Now

Russ Burnett, the program director at KMPC, the all-time most popular personality station in Los Angeles history, called me one afternoon to ask if I'd like to work for him.

He said he had heard me on KGBS after listening to one of the dozens of tapes I'd sent him, and that he would like to develop me into a KMPC personality. To start with, though, all he could offer was vacation relief and weekends.

KMPC was *the* station in L.A., starring Dick Whittinghill, Geoff Edwards, Wink Martindale, Gary Owens, Roger Carrol, Johnny Magnus, and Clark Race. "God, how could a chump like me get a job on KMPC," I thought as all my years of doubt kicked in. "But maybe this time I can be somebody."

My heart was pumping in my eyes again. KMPC was Gene Autry's station. Without a doubt, it was every radio personality's dream radio station. All the talent on the station made big money. It was an unbelievable operation, and they wanted me.

In addition to the top radio guys working there, KMPC carried the Los Angeles Rams games, Angel's Baseball, and UCLA Football. I was hired just about the time the Carpenter's "Close to You" was a monster hit.

I asked Russ if it would be possible to work for KMPC *and* KGBS until some other opportunities came up at KMPC. He said it would be all right by him if Roger Christian didn't mind. When I told Roger about it, he grinned widely and then hugged me and told me he that he figured someone would grab me up.

"You're going to have a fabulous career in radio," he said, and then he insisted I work at KMPC and KGBS until things played out. What a great guy. That year I had another first: I was invited to be one of the emcees at the famous Hollywood Santa Claus Parade down Hollywood Blvd. Am I somebody yet?

Working at KMPC was tremendous. The studios were on Sunset Blvd., right next to the Hollywood Freeway, and they were state of the art. There were three on-air studios, all built just alike, and each one was sitting on a floating foundation to keep them from jarring during an earthquake. It was an incredible set up. Ron Landry wrote some liners for me the first night I sat in for Johnny Magnus. What a rush—KMPC.

It was the fall of 1969. Thanksgiving was only a few weeks away, and Gene Autry made it a point to come to the station personally and show his appreciation. Mr. Autry gave everyone a turkey and a ham for Thanksgiving.

After a couple of weeks working for Johnny Magnus while he was at the Brazilian Music Fest in Rio de Janeiro, I filled in on the all-night show. The next morning when Dick Whittinghill came in, he said, "Great show kid. You sound super."

I felt like I had arrived. Whittinghill, one of my idols, was famous in Los Angeles radio. What a station. Gary Owens was the guy on "Laugh In" with his hand cuffed over his ear. Martindale was also a well-known game show host. What a lineup—now Brad Edwards.

I didn't feel like somebody yet, but it was good. I was just the "fill-in" guy. "Don't get too excited," I thought. Always in the back of my mind was the thought that it could all disappear in a heartbeat.

After a year, when I was really digging being the only guy in town who worked for two great radio stations at once, Roger called me at the house to tell me something was up.

"I want you to go with me to take over a new station," he told me. "You'll be my operations director and do middays."

Roger was my man. I believed in him, so when he said let's take our act to Mexico, I said, "Si, Senor." Adios KGBS and KMPC. The most difficult station to leave was KMPC, where I'd been for about a year and was hoping to become a regular. Roger said he needed my full attention. Oh well; that's radio.

Chapter 20
Let's Hear It for the Wolfman

A couple of investors had bought XERB where Wolfman Jack had migrated, broadcasting from Ciudad Acuna on XERF, a 150,000 watt border monster there.

John Herklotz, who had been the comptroller for WGN in Chicago for many years, had teamed up with a couple of attorney's and bought the sales rights from the Mexicans. That meant that he and his partners controlled the programming and sales on the station.

Herklotz was an extraordinary man, brilliant with numbers, and an out-of-the-box thinker. We would work together for most of my radio career in one way or another. It was he, ultimately, who gave me the opportunity to really be somebody.

The XeRB call letters were changed to XePRS or "Express." Roger tried to get the owners to change the name from XeRB to XeLAX, but they just laughed. What rapid recognition that set of call letters would have received as folks tuned in to hear Wolfman Jack on ExLax.

Our studios were in Hollywood, and the XePRS transmitter was located in Roserito Beach, Mexico. It was very powerful and could be heard from Mexico City to Nome, Alaska. Roserito Beach, Mexico is between Tijuana and Ensenada, about thirty miles south of "TJ" in Baja, California.

The Mexican's were very proud of their station. It was on a hillside overlooking Roserito Beach itself. It came complete with a fully functional studio that had a panoramic view of the Pacific Ocean. The floor of the transmitter was made up of small mosaic tiles, the most beautiful transmitter site I had ever seen.

As director of operations, this was my first management job, and I was anxious to do everything right. Part of my job description included keeping an eye on Wolfman Jack when he was in our studios, in order to keep him from stealing stuff, or as the Wolf liked to put it, "Borrowing a few things for a couple of days."

Wolfman had his own studios in the Hollywood Hills where he and his wife, Lu, lived. Wolf was on the air from 9:00 PM until midnight on the station. I loved the guy, but occasionally he needed things to keep his studio going and wasn't shy about "borrowing" them from our Hollywood studios.

Wolfman, or Bob Smith, which was his real name, was really on a natural high. He had just completed *American Graffiti* and was reveling in the stardom. He took everything a day at a time and simply enjoyed wallowing in the limelight.

Wolf and his entourage came to the station one afternoon, joking, laughing, and being the "star" that he was when all of a sudden, I noticed that one of our stand-up Ampex tape recorders was missing. It was a major piece of equipment. I just happened to glance into the studio and saw the empty spot it left and the impression in the carpet where the wheels had rested.

He kept everyone laughing in Roger's office while his producer, Lonnie, slipped out the back with it. I ran outside just as Lonnie and another ne'r-do-well were loading it in their van.

"We're just borrowing it for a couple of days," Lonnie explained. "Wolf's machine crapped out."

Just then, Wolfman Jack stepped out.

"Ah, come on, Bradley. I'll bring it back, man," he growled at me in his famous voice that sounded like he had just gargled with ground glass.

"Oh, all right," I consented.

So I let him have it "for a couple of days," and it only took me six weeks to get it back. Usually when Wolf borrowed something, you'd get it back, but it wasn't exactly the same piece of equipment that he had initially borrowed.

"Express" was a good station, but the owners had the misguided notion that they could get away with calling it "A One Station West Coast Network." Our coverage map included: San Diego, Los Angeles, and San Francisco.

They bought into the notion that we could claim those markets and go after that ad revenue. The problem was that while we scored very well in San Diego, our daytime signal skirted Los Angeles and was practically non-existent in San Francisco.

Now at night, we could claim the entire West Coast, minus Los Angeles and San Francisco, because we "skipped over" or "skirted" around them. Name a city in Oregon, Washington, Canada, or Alaska, though, and we put a signal in there, once the sun went down.

Roger was quick to recognize that San Diego should be the target. He suggested that we move the offices to San Diego—since we had the highest ratings in that city—and that we should do our shows from Roserito Beach. The suits in the front office, however, except for Herklotz, wanted to keep things as they were, so it only took a year or so for the station to start slipping.

Chapter 21
Minnesota Brad!

Next door to our Hollywood studios was a billiard parlor/ sandwich and beer bar. It was cool and hip and became my hangout after work. There must have been fifteen or twenty pool tables for any variety of games: snooker, billiards, eight ball, nine ball—you name it.

It was so nice, in fact, that the Grey Advertising Media Pool Tournament was held there that year. Grey was a very successful ad firm responsible for a wide array of extraordinarily creative radio, TV, and print ads.

It was a Friday night. My day was done, and I had registered for the tourney, so I went next door to practice and have a couple of beers. "A couple of beers" is, of course, only a euphemism for "as many beers as I can drink and still manage to remain standing."

There was an AE (account executive) with Grey who won the nine-ball competition every year. He was a wise ass. I didn't like the guy because he was sarcastic, arrogant, and spoke down to everyone. Not a good thing for a guy like me who operated in the low-self-esteem zone. I was thinking, "I'm fifty times as good looking as this chump, so I'll psyche him out with that." It's amazing, actually, how that works on some guys.

So, the inferiority complex was kicking in, but the ego maniac in me was pressing on. I was feeling no pain when the tournament began. I won the first required preliminary games in the eight ball competition but lost in the next, so I was out of that portion of the tourney, though I was still signed up for the nine ball competition.

I had a couple more beers and noticed that the sales guy from Grey was strutting his stuff. He was a blustery jag-off, and he got to me a little, but I could do no wrong that night. I was half drunk and in the middle of the nine ball competition and kickin' ass. Minnesota Fats couldn't have touched me that night. My stick was humming.

I worked my way up the brackets until it was just me and the guy from Grey.

"You're not going to be able to pull that shit on me," he said, referring to a masse shot that I had pulled off while playing a guy from KHJ.

I just looked at him and smiled. Pure and simple, it was the best nine ball I ever played. I was in way over my head, but "Screw it, I can beat this chump," said the booze.

I thought back to when I was in the sixth grade. The school bully at Riverside grade school in Grants Pass, Oregon, a big clod, had tried to pick a fight with me and was caught in the act by Coach Thomas.

"You boys aren't going to fight," Coach had said. "You're going to compete."

He asked Roy, the bully, to pick his favorite competition.

"Shot put?" he ventured.

"Oh, man!" I thought. This guy out-weighed me by fifty pounds, and his arms were as big around as my thighs. I was a skinny kid, tall and gangly. "Thanks, Coach." I thought. "Now I'm screwed, and in front of everybody."

As Roy was setting up the put, I was thinking, "Oh God," how can I compete with this gorilla?" I told the bully, "Don't fart when you throw the putt." Everyone laughed and it pissed him off, which is what I wanted. I was always a wise guy when I was nervous. He groaned, and then threw that put way out there, though not as far as I thought he would. My comment had gotten to him.

Everyone was always scared around that clown because he picked on us. He was big as a house and had an IQ of about forty. I don't know why I wisecracked to him. "It's just something else to make him pound harder when he's beating on me," I thought.

Now, it was my turn. I overheard Coach Thomas quietly tell one of the teachers' standing next to him, "Watch this. Claude will beat him by two feet." I spun around, roaring as I called on every adrenalin-activated muscle in my body, and heaved that put in great Olympic style and beat the peckerwood by a good foot and a half. It was a miracle.

I seemed to be able to pull something from somewhere I didn't know existed. That would be a good thing for me over the years, as I was about to find out in the pool hall. I felt then, like I was feeling right now, faced with this wise guy from Grey.

I won the first break and he never got a shot. I ran the table on him. I put on a nine-ball showcase for the remainder of the competition.

As they handed me the trophy, I could hear him sniveling to a couple of his buddies, "The guy's drunk on his ass." He belched.

I turned, held the trophy outstretched in his direction, and said, "Good game. Maybe next time you'll get a few more shots."

Express radio was running into deep trouble. The owners were quibbling about sales. There were not enough commercials to pay for the operation. Roger tried again to get the owners to move to San Diego, but two of the three owners were still stuck on that West-Coast network crap.

When they fired Rog, I told John Herklotz, the partner in favor of moving to San Diego, that I'd be moving on. I believed in Rog, and I didn't like the way he was being treated, especially in light of the fact that he couldn't possibly get ratings for the station in an area where it couldn't be heard.

Chapter 22
Break Out the Mobile Zip Code Again

Herklotz asked me to stay at XePRS, but I declined; besides, I was being courted by Arnie Shore, who managed a successful urban-formatted station in Los Angeles called KGFJ.

More importantly, Shore's company was buying an FM, and they were about to launch a new format that would be fresh and innovative. He offered me the morning show on what became known as KUTE 102, which covered all of Southern California, from Los Angeles to San Diego.

KUTE 102 was an odd radio station. First of all, the format was an Urban Album Radio format, playing upcoming and secondary tracks from a variety of R&B artists, but not the commercial singles that you'd find on, say, our urban station KGFJ. Actually, it was refreshing and different, but what was odd is that the station was located in a Lilly White suburb of Los Angeles called Glendale, and the air staff was totally white too.

I was the morning man and Chris Roberts was on afternoons. Chris is now the voice of the UCLA Bruins. Remind me to tell you about the time he threw his golf club up in a tree so high that he had to climb up about fifty feet to get it down, in front of everyone in the clubhouse, as it was on the eighteenth green. Chris and I were able to get Jhani Kaye hired. I was a guest teacher at a broadcasting school in Los Angeles and was fortunate to have Jhani, an extraordinary talent, as a student. In the early '70s, Jhani followed in my and Chris Roberts footsteps and became a DJ on KFXM in San Bernardino, after paying his dues in Hemet, California. There, the average listener is about ninety years old. Later, Jhani became the premiere Adult Contemporary programmer in the U.S., taking KFI and KOST FM in Los Angeles to great success.

A couple of years later when I was back at KGBS, Jhani lost his gig at KUTE 102, and I recommended that they hire him at my station. It was at KGBS that Jhani came to me and said he'd been offered something that would change his career choice.

"It's as program director for KINT 98 FM in El Paso, Texas," he said. Jhani had long been a wizard with music and research.

"Hell, yes!" I told him. "This is what you were made to do in radio."

Jhani is a great guy and wonderful programmer. He took the job, but it took him off the air.

Also on the staff at KUTE 102 was one of the greatest guys and extraordinary talents I've ever known: Bill Stevens, who did middays. Bill and I, oddly, have been on what might be called a parallel existence in our lives. Bill and I have the same birthday—October eleventh—and although Bill is about five years younger than myself, we both graduated from Montebello High School in Los Angeles. After high school, I went to work for Raheb Film Labs in Hollywood, processing films and mixing the processing chemicals. A few years later, so did Bill. Coincidence? I don't know.

Years later when the KUTE 102 party was over, Bill bought a sail boat and navigated himself down to the islands of American Samoa, the Marquesas, Bora Bora, Tahiti, and became the general manager of a radio station on American Samoa for about six months. Radio will take you where you want to go, and sometimes, where you don't want to be.

"Death was a big deal to Samoans," he said, laughing. "One of the big customs on the island was to buy five-minute eulogies for the dearly departed. I'd be playing something by the Stones, come to a stop set, and read a eulogy along with the dead recipient's favorite musical selection."

Hilarious!

On his way back, south west of Hawaii, he had to navigate his small sailboat through a hellacious storm, but not without tying himself to the craft to prevent himself from being washed overboard. Bill said it was phenomenal, with waves so high that he'd be going straight up one moment, and then straight down the next. He made it home, with enough stories to last a lifetime.

Somehow, we both ended up at KFXM in San Bernardino in 1966. I was on the air afternoons and Bill was the midday guy. Bill is the prototype of what Boss Radio was looking for. He had the best, smoothest, warmest presentation I've ever heard. He presented a flawless dance over the lips of records and never made a mistake.

Chapter 23

It Was Majic

I received a call from Jim Maddox, who was a big tall brother, about six foot six, I think. Maddox was moving on a fast track in L.A. radio, and he told me he was between gigs and had developed a new format. He asked if I'd let him work on the prototype in the production room at KUTE early in the morning while I was on the air.

"Come on over, Jim," I told him.

Maddox was different. He was a nonconformist, and I'd have the opportunity to be associated with him for years after that. He was my kind of guy. He thought so far out of the box that simply the freshness of his thinking was enjoyable.

His idea was a new urban format that he started at KDAY in Los Angeles, a big 50,000-watt station not far from KUTE. The name of his format was "Majic," with a J. He asked me what I thought of the sound, and it did sound incredibly hip.

It was a mix of urban songs, with the likes of Johnny Taylor or the Blackbirds, along with soft jazz like Herbie Hancock or Grover Washington, and a few white artists crossing over like Bobby Caldwell, who sang "What You Won't do For Love."

Majic was "smoother than a pocket full of warm butterscotch," as my old friend and mentor Emperor Hudson would say. He took a few chances with his music too; one of my favorites was "I Should Have Loved You" by Narada Michael Walden.

I would find out later, while doing mornings for Maddox at a couple of stations, that his system was difficult to implement while you were on the air. You practically had to have a degree in music rotation to qualify the next record you played.

It was almost impossible to mix together like he envisioned it, especially for a morning guy who has so many other ingredients he's concerned with during morning drive, like traffic, weather, and personality thoughts—stuff like that.

Jim pulled me in to KDAY where the money was real good after I left KUTE 102. What a mess it was, but we turned it around. To make a long story short, we took the station to number *one* in Los Angeles in a very short time, which was a phenomenal accomplishment. It was one of AM radio's last big grunts in Los Angeles.

Management meddled with the format too much though, so Jim left and I was recruited back to KGBS just about the time it went to a new format called "Gentle Country."

Maddox was only able to implement some of his ideas at KDAY, so he moved on to Houston for his first bona fide success with Majic. I would work for his St. Louis station, Majic 108, and then move on to Houston later to be the morning guy on Jim's Flagship, Majic 102.

"What the heck is 'Gentle Country?'" I thought. Well, it was a modern update to country music and included some folks like

John Denver, with songs like "Thank God I'm a Country Boy" and "Rocky Mountain High," The Bellamy Brothers, and many traditional artists as well.

I don't know if it was the country music or having to play "My Pet Rock" one more time, or maybe it was listening to Jimmy Carter talk about what was going on in Plains, Georgia, but I took a rest from working on my show for awhile and just concentrated on drinking.

It was doable working afternoons. I could drink all night and sleep 'til noon. I didn't have to prepare a lot for an afternoon show, where it was simply play the hits and talk in between records. Hard drinking was my way of life at the time.

Chapter 24
Hello, Bill W.

Life was beginning to turn around for me. I did very well on KGBS, and I didn't want to lose the job because of my drinking. I was told about a psychologist who was a rising star treating Hollywood stars, helping them with their alcohol and drug problems. His office was in downtown Hollywood.

Dr. Wilbert Greenbaum was a tall, gray-haired man, a bit on the thin side. He was a warm, but "down to business." He looked like he was constantly taking mental notes, which, of course, he was.

I spent two sessions with Dr. Greenbaum as he took notes on my history.

On the third visit, he said, "I believe I can help you, but before we can continue, you have go to a meeting of alcoholics, tonight."

"Of alcoholics?" I said like I had been insulted. "Do you think I'm an alcoholic?" Ha ha. What a joke. I was getting drunk every other day now and I honestly questioned his diagnosis.

"There's more to it than that, though," Greenbaum said. "We need to find out what's going on inside your head."

"What do you want from me?" he asked.

"I want to stop drinking and be released from the obsession to chase women so much," I told him—not completely, but mostly.

"The drinking and the women?" he said. "That's what I'm talking about. There's more inside your head, and we'll find out what it is."

I made that first meeting with the alcoholics on Ohio Street in Santa Monica that night. There was trouble right off the bat. The first guy I ran into was a guy whose wife I had hit on a couple of years before. I felt terrible, and his AA buddies had to hold him back from kicking my ass. I was off to a bad start, but I was determined to keep coming back.

He and his wife broke up, so one night, on one of my drunken, "cruise 'til you get laid" trips around town, I called her and asked if I could come over. She didn't want anything to do with me, but he didn't know that. The wreckage of my past was catching up with me.

The meetings with Dr. Greenbaum were going well. I also talked Arlene into joining me in marriage group therapy, which, to my astonishment, she consented to. Finally, after all these years, I was beginning to reap the benefits of getting my life together.

I noticed that a calmness was coming over me. It was a stillness that I had never experienced. I was spilling the beans to Greenbaum and getting a lot off my chest.

In marriage group, Arlene was having difficulty sharing anything, let alone anything constructive. It was just the way she was. She kept it all inside. We were drifting further apart from one another, so any hope for a normal relationship was diminishing.

During one personal session with me, Dr. Greenbaum said,

"Tell me what happened to you when you were a boy."

"How could he know?" I thought, though I said, "What do you mean?"

"Something happened to you that you're keeping secret," he said, searching.

Oh, God. I mumbled out that something happened in Grants Pass when I was about ten years old.

"What happened" he gently prodded.

"Uh, something that I got myself into by being so stupid," I began. "I … I went out to the carnival that was in town. We boys would regularly go to events like that and help the ride operators set things up. We'd get free ride passes and stuff. I was helping this guy who operated a kiddies ride get set up."

I told Dr. Greenbaum the entire horrible story, in every detail. I sobbed the entire time, but I couldn't stop now, all the years of stuffing it away inside were over. After about thirty minutes of testimony about the worst day of my life, Dr. Greenbaum hugged me like a father—the father who wasn't there for me when I went through the nightmare the first horrific time.

I loved him for that. I told Dr. Greenbaum about the authorities having let the bastard go, and how my mother encouraged me to try to put the episode behind me. I told him how my dad had called me a queer, and then rejected me completely. How he walked away for my entire life. I was devastated, and I could tell that Dr. Greenbaum had a difficult time with it too.

I sat in Dr. Greenbaum's office that day crying quietly, not realizing that my life would begin to change dramatically, very soon. I had been relieved of the bondage of the guilt and responsibility of that rape, which I can't call "molestation" because it is what it is.

Molestation is an inappropriate word that doesn't adequately describe the ferocious reality of the crime. It should be characterized as the vicious raping of a young boy. Molestation makes it sound like there was maybe some inappropriate touching involved.

All the emotion that went into thinking that somehow it was my fault was drained from me that afternoon. I spent all those years trying to prove my father wrong about my manliness. I know that explanation is an over simplification, but that's how it started. That's how I felt as a young man.

It took awhile, but eventually my feelings about women would begin to change. No longer would they be objects to complete my maleness. I would learn to enjoy women as genuine friends and colleagues whom I cared for and liked being with, far from the realm of sexuality. It was a slow process, but truly a gift from God.

Soon, it became apparent to me that Arlene was locked up in her secret world. So, finally, we broke up, once and for all. There's little doubt that I probably drove her into the hard shell she hid in. No woman in the world deserved to be treated the way I had treated her.

I was drunk several times a week and went home from the bars with whoever would take me. The best thing that ever happened to Arlene was getting rid of the loser of a husband that I had been from the very beginning.

One of the few positive results from those years were my two daughters, Cindi and Melissa. As children, they never saw me drunk, and I rarely raised my voice to them, and never my hand. I just wasn't always there. I always treated them with all my love and care, and I still love them with all my heart.

When I sat my two daughters down, along with Arlene, and told them, "Daddy is going to live somewhere else for awhile," the shock on my two girl's faces almost made me burst out in tears.

"Will Missy and I still get to live together?" Cindi asked. This told me that she thought that the baby was my favorite and that I'd split them up, which was absolutely not so. I was crazy about both of them.

"My God!" I thought. "What am I doing to my family?" I was completely distraught. Arlene knew it was coming, but the impact on my girls was devastating. That was, without a doubt, the most heartbreaking afternoon of my life.

I was convinced that even if I were sober, I wouldn't want to be married to Arlene. She, on the other hand, had every reason in the world to not want anything to do with me, yet she wanted to keep trying. It's all there in the Al-anon handbook.

I had finally gone to my program for alcoholics in February of 1975 and had somehow stayed sober for several months. My behavior changed a lot, and my boss gave me special perks whenever he could. Nice strokes, pats on the back, and he even pressed the Academy of Country Music to nominate me as "Major Market Personality of The Year." I still don't know if he really did or not, but he said I was nominated two years in a row. I just wasn't happy working country music and the accolades didn't matter to me.

Chapter 25
Strike Three

I don't know if it was the day-to-day pressures of life, or merely the fact that, because I'm an alcoholic, I just wanted to drink, but eventually I went back to drinking. Later, my sponsor, Ernie, would clear up what it takes to make me drink.

"If anything will make you drink, anything will make you drink," he said. Very profound.

I waited until I was on vacation. That way, hopefully, no one would know about it. Step aside, I'm headed downhill, but not before I drink my way around South America. A month-long trip to Panama, Caracas, Rio de Janeiro, Montevideo, Buenos Aires, Santiago, Lima, Quito, Bogotá, and then back to Panama to meet up with Heidi, the Pan Am stewardess I met on the way down.

I barely remember any of it because I was in a continuous blackout. I do remember being halfway over the Amazon from Caracas to Rio when an engine in the Pan Am 747 we were on blew out. I froze up.

The pilot came on and told us we were headed back to Venezuela to get a new plane. We didn't know how serious it was until we saw all the fire trucks, safety vehicles, and personnel lined up along the runway as we landed.

When I got back to the states, I tried to hide my drinking, and was successful for almost a year. I had a very nice apartment in Playa del Rey. It was my first year as a single man, and I handled it pretty well, but I was lonely.

My soul was still empty. Chasing women didn't satisfy my manliness like it used to. I wanted someone to love, really love. It was a new emotion. I finally realized that a new corner of my brain had opened up. I wanted someone to lie next to and trade dreams with, to hold, kiss, and tease. I didn't know how to accomplish this. Dr. Greenbaum didn't tell me there would be days like this.

Radio was headed in a phenomenally high-tech direction, so automation was finding its way on the air because of it. Prior to that time, you could easily tell when a disc jockey was not actually there, but KGBS was experimenting with a new automation system and we were all getting nervous.

Ron Martin, our Operations Director, had tried to take me under his wing. He was aware that I had fallen off the wagon, and he knew that my drinking would be a problem if he kept me.

So, I was about to lose my first job on account of drinking. Ron couldn't count on me, my few friends couldn't count on me, and I couldn't count on me. Faced with automation and cutting his staff back to a couple of people, Ron had to make some choices, and I wasn't one of them.

One of my friends on the air at KGBS was Michael Hunter. He was our midday DJ. When he got off at noon, we'd drive over to El Cholo restaurant on South Western in Hollywood and drink lunch.

It was a very cool restaurant, and they had several little Mexican idioms carved into the wall: "No llores, hay mas peces en el mar," which means "Don't cry, there are more fish in the sea," and "En boca cerado, no entran las moscas," meaning "Keep your mouth shut and no flies will go in."

We'd head over there and plan our futures, knowing that our days were numbered at Storer Broadcasting. Michael was friends with Claude Hall, of *Billboard* magazine, which was, at that time, the industry bible for radio and recording.

Claude mentioned to Michael that the Iranian government was looking for two U.S. disc jockey's to fill slots on their National Iranian Radio & Television Network (NIRT) in Tehran. It was a far-reaching radio station that served English-speaking people working in Iran. NIRT could be heard all over the country, in Tehran, Isfahan, Tabriz, and even up to the Caspian Sea.

Michael asked if I'd be interested. We discussed it over a couple of huge margaritas at El Cholo and decided that it would be fun. It paid over six figures and had many perks that looked attractive.

Part of the deal was that every six months we could go anywhere we wanted for five days with free passage on Iran Air. We thought that would be great.

Later, we were less than enthusiastic about flying Iran Air when we discovered that the planes were put in the air with spit and duct tape—junk. Anyway, Claude said he would set up a meeting with Iran's agent to see if we could work it out.

It was almost Christmas of 1976 when Claude Hall got back to us to say that he had recommended the two of us to Kamron Mashyekhi, who was the Shah of Iran's representative for the National Iranian Radio & Television Network.

We spoke with Kamron over the phone several times and came to a verbal agreement. We'd go to Iran, Michael would program NIRT, I would do the midday show from noon to 5:00 PM, and Michael would play the heavy rock and roll from 5:00 to 10:00 PM.

Michael had been the program director and morning man for KMET in Los Angeles during the heyday of album rock and was a walking almanac of rock and roll. He was a handsome guy with a very ballsy voice that the women loved. Michael was about five foot ten, with brown hair, and he wore round, wireless glasses like John Lennon. His facial features were quite interesting. He was strikingly handsome, with big, warm blue eyes, and when he spoke, a rich, friendly person took command.

Michael drove a Porsche, and I had a Jaguar XKE that Roger Christian, my mentor, who wrote so many racing hits for the Beach Boys and Jan and Dean, had talked me into buying. He told me it was just like the one he had in mind when he wrote "Dead Man's Curve," which was a premonition of the accident that would almost kill Jan of Jan and Dean.

My XKE was baby blue with a deep blue leather interior, and a five-speed stick that could really crank. I had her up past 120 mph more than once, and that was on the Hollywood freeway. We'd have to put both cars in storage, not to mention all our other belongings, but it would be worth it. They were going to pay us very well.

Sure enough, it was Christmas and KGBS let Michael and I go. Screw it. I told Michael that until we heard from Claude Hall, I would be in Europe. I took off for England.

Chapter 26
Adrift Again, Ooh La La

I caught an overnight flight to London out of Los Angeles. By the time we landed at Heathrow, it was a little after five in the morning. It was snowing. I was tired and hit the sack in my room at a hotel in Piccadilly Square right away.

That night at the pub in the hotel, I met a beautiful Russian girl named Alexis. She was from St. Petersburg and was incredibly gorgeous. She had blonde hair, blue eyes, and a sensuous Russian accent that whispered from two beautifully full, soft lips. When she spoke, she touched me softly with her fingertips, and I liked that. When I met her, she was wearing a Sable coat that was puffy in the arms and tight at the waist.

She worked for the Russian consulate as a translator. Hell, she may have been a spy for that matter, but it didn't concern me. Anything I held secret, the Ruskies wouldn't be interested in.

As we were exchanging pleasantries over a cocktail, an English couple joined us at our table. The two of them were standing in the crowded room holding their drinks and talking, so I motioned for them to join us and they did.

It was very European as we acquainted ourselves with one another. They were from Manchester. He was an airline pilot spending a few days with his wife in London. He was tall, with light-brown hair and droopy eyes that seemed to match his matter-of-fact English accent.

She was cute with a head full of short, dark curls that looked like each one was about to spring out. She had a smile that seemed to have more lips than were needed for the job and she laughed at everything.

It was nice, and Alexis was having fun. We thoroughly enjoyed the exchange and I was able to forget, for the moment at least, that I didn't have much of a future. Three days later, I kissed Alexis goodbye and took off for Copenhagen.

As the BOAC jet lifted off, I felt an incredible sense of satisfaction. Alexis had been very good for me. It was one of the first times in my life when I felt vulnerable with a woman. Was I changing? I would miss her.

On the plane to Paris I met Klaus. Klaus was from Berlin, and he had moved to Paris to work for a group of fashion designers, directing sales for their lines all over Europe. He was rather short, with curly brown hair and had a terrific personality.

The flight to Paris was a short one but in that time we struck up a friendship. I told him that I was staying at the Sheraton in Paris and he urged me to spend at least the first night in a hotel that he said was Old Europe. A hotel, he said that would give me the flavor of the real Paris.

It was on the Left Bank and was the Hotel des Deux Continents. It was in the heart of the Saint Germain de Pres district. The minute we arrived at Orly, he went to a pay phone and made the arrangements.

The following night was his wife's birthday, and he insisted that I come to the party and spend the night.

Before he left, he wrote out directions in French to his home in the Paris suburbs and said to give it to the cab driver, who'd know what to do.

"One more thing, my American friend," he said as he was leaving. "Only a few blocks from the Hotel des Deux Continents is a restaurant called Aux Assassin, on Rue Jacob. It is there you should have dinner tonight to feel ze French life."

With that advice, he was off. I had a friend and directions to Hotel des Deux Continent.

What an extraordinary little hotel. It was small, with a foyer that had a small coffee table, with a few soft chairs on either side, and a plant stuffed in between them in a very crowded but comfortable look.

At the front desk, I found a well-dressed old man, complete with WWII medals and ribbons draped on his evening jacket, an ascot, and wad of colorful silk hanging out of his pocket. he even looked a little like Charles DeGaule. He spoke no English and I spoke no French, but somehow we got the registration done. My room was atop a beautiful winding staircase that was straight out of nineteenth-century Europe. In the room there was a small circular window where I could see the lights along the Seine. The small bathroom was almost antique and very clean.

Even though the room was small, the bed was large and it had an extra large down blanket spread over it that looked like it was a foot thick. It made a warm and comfortable addition for such a cold night. Klaus was right. I could check in at the Sheraton later. Right now, I was in Old Europe.

I cleaned up, and it was only nine o'clock, so I bounded down the spiral staircase, which by the way could only accommodate one person at a time, and asked the old man at the desk if he had heard of Aux Assassin. He smiled and pointed east. I walked east along the Seine, which to me was incredible. I had heard of this wonderful place all my life, and now I was here, walking along the most famous river in France. Boats, lit up and loaded with partying people, cruised up and down the river. I felt lonely right then, wondering if I would ever have someone to love, hold, and enjoy.

The Cathedral du Notre Dame was not far from where I was walking. The air was cold, but fresh. I don't know how, but within a few minutes of stumbling along Rue Jacob, I found myself inside the Aux Assassin restaurant.

The Aux Assassin was an interesting place. The restaurant was very busy. There were big, long tables where you sat next to strangers and ate, drank, and enjoyed their company. It was cool. I was well dressed and hoped to say the right thing at the right time. Well, I would have, but not a word of English was spoken. Ha ha. It was hilarious.

The waiters laughed and gestured with me, and even tried to introduce me to the young ladies, who were there in abundance. I was a word merchant without a word to sell. I drank some red wine, ordered some spaghetti and meatballs, and started tearing the bread apart like everyone else.

I noticed that two unescorted young ladies across the table were checking me out. I smiled and nodded. They offered me a flirtatious return.

The French I had studied in college before I switched to Spanish was worthless.

"American?" the brunette asked. What a beautiful word when said with a French accent.

"Oui," I replied.

"Parlez-vous Française?" she queried.

"No," I answered apologetically, wishing I had stuck with the French classes. The three of us just stared at each other, offering smiles.

"Me nom is Claude." I said.

Here I was, a Yankee with a French name, and I could barely say a word in their language. No wonder the French are so nasty to us. The sweetheart with the dark hair introduced herself as Dominique. She had soft-looking skin that appeared as if she had just gotten out of a long, hot bath.

Her friend had dishwater blond hair, very sexy green oval eyes, perhaps a bit too much make-up, but was sexy nevertheless. With the exception of her Charles De Gaulle nose, she was attractive. I was thinking that there had to be a way to get to know them.

After a few clumsy wine toasts and some vain attempts at speaking French with my hands as interpreters, and them trying their best with the few English words they knew, I said, "Habla español?"

Dominique's eyes lit up and she said, "Si, hablo español. Como estas, Claude?" A breakthrough.

My years of Spanish had finally paid off. It was tough on Michelle, though, but we all communicated. Dominique was a pharmacist, and Michelle worked for France Radio One in promotions. Radio One was a famous radio organization in Paris. How ironic that we were both in the radio business and I couldn't even talk to her about it.

She was very curious about my radio career, but unfortunately, I was more interested in pharmacy at the moment. We laughed and drank for hours until it was time to go. We arranged a double date for Saturday night. Michelle would be with Henri, a pharmaceutical salesman that Dominique knew, and we would do the town.

The ladies dropped me off at Deux Continent. As I stepped from the car, Dominique, who was driving, jumped out and said, "Claude."

She put her hands behind the back of my head and gently kissed me full on the lips.

"Au revoir, mon cherie," she said.

I kind of wished that I hadn't told Klaus that I'd be there for his wife's birthday the next night, as I would much rather have spent Friday night with Dominique, but "c'est la vie."

Alas, it's Friday now and I'm in a cab trying to get the driver to interpret Klaus's directions. We drove out to some beautiful homes in the suburbs and finally located Klaus's place, a gorgeous old French Villa. I thought, "The boy's doing all right."

I thought everyone had a villa in France. I stepped inside; the door was open and the party was on.

"Claude, how are you my friend?" Klaus asked, greeting me like I was a long-lost friend.

I had mentioned to Klaus that I worked for a radio station in Los Angeles that was an NBC affiliate, so he told everyone at the party that his friend from NBC in the States was dropping by for Inga's birthday party.

It was a small party of about fifteen people, mostly French, and a couple from Belgium, a German and his wife, and the birthday girl, Inga. She was from East Germany and looked like she was glad to be living anywhere else but there. She had curly dark brown hair, tight to her head and kind of pulled back on one side. She was very attractive, seductive, and was maybe five foot seven. "Klaus is a lucky man," I thought. Inga had been a runway model whom Klaus had met in his work.

The spotlight was on me. I had become friends with Don Sutton, a pitcher for the Los Angeles Dodgers who had his hair permed. He in turn talked me into having my hair curled as well. It was a fad in the mid-to-late '70s, so I decided to try it. It looked pretty good.

It seems that it hadn't caught on in Europe, though, because all the women at the party couldn't resist touching it and rubbing their fingers through it. The Belgian wife not only ran her fingers through it, she whispered something in French close to my ear and grabbed a handful of my ass. A little crude, I thought, but everyone had a buzz on, and I liked the attention.

It was a typical birthday party, and Klaus's wife, Inga, was having a ball. I thought *I* could drink. Man, those Frenchmen drank nonstop. I slowed down with some French beer, which Klaus referred to in his delightful accent as "piss beer." He said that all it was good for was "one piss after another piss and you are not to feel the buzz." He was right.

It was getting late, and Inga had fixed up one of her kid's rooms for me. They had sent the children off to stay with relatives for a few days so that they could have the house to themselves.

As I lay down on the miniature bed, my feet hung off the end of it, but it was doable. It had been a nice party and I was looking forward to my date with Dominique the following night.

I had just drifted off when suddenly I felt someone in the room with me. It was Inga, and she was kneeling next to the bed with her hand on my manhood.

Oh, God! How do I handle this? Klaus's wife? What little control I had over my inhibitions was being challenged. I was slipping, but I grabbed her by her curly head and whispered, "Inga, I can't do this." She looked up at me, smiled, and continued what she was doing; I guess she was having a hard time deciphering my English.

I was losing the battle, but I made one more attempt. She then stopped, stood up, and pulled off her panties, straddling me as I lay there. I was done for.

She fell into my arms, kissing me and breathing heavily into a passionate crescendo. She said in her broken German accent, "Sank you, Claude, for ziz beautiful birthday present."

It was difficult to figure out. The next morning, Klaus gave me a little tour, driving us through Versailles, past L'Arc de Triomphe and down along the Champs Elysee and eventually back to the Hotel des Deux Continent.

Finally, we shook hands to say goodbye and he said,

"Merci, mon ami. Inga will always remember this birthday."

It finally hit me. Klaus had brought me home for his wife's birthday—as a present. Damn, if I had figured it out earlier, I might have enjoyed it a little more.

Chapter 27
When in Paris

When Dominique introduced me to Henri, I thought he was extremely cool. He was one of the most handsome guys I'd ever met, like a young Cary Grant. I imagined he made a lot of guys uneasy when he was around. He had jet-black hair, and was about my height of six foot one. He looked somewhat like Pierce Brosnan too, but was totally French. Thank God he spoke English, even though he had a thick French accent. I enjoyed his great sense of humor as well.

As a pharmaceutical drug manufacturer's rep, he spent a lot of time in the Middle East, especially Beirut. Knowing that Dominique and Michelle couldn't speak English, he honed in on my American sense of humor, referring occasionally to Michelle as,

"An incredible blowjob, Claude."

I had to stifle my laugh lest they catch on that Henri was poking fun, so to speak.

"Big nose, great blowjob, Claude." I would just look at her when he was referring to her and smile as though he had said something complementary, which, really, he had.

We went to Harry's New York Bar in Paris. Harry's had long been frequented by famous people and was a favorite of Ernest Hemingway, Italian conductor Arturo Toscanini, radio pioneer Guglielmo Marconi, Charlie Chaplin, Truman Capote, Orson Wells, and even Woody Allen, to name a few.

I think it's important to remember the place where the first hot dog in France was served in 1925. Also, what they drank could be found nowhere else. It was here that drinks like the Bloody Mary were born. The start of Harry's tradition goes back to 1923, when a Scott named Harry MacElhone, fresh from a stint as bartender at Ciro's Club in London, took over what was known as the New York Bar in Paris.

Henri told me that it was Harry's Bar that started the tradition of insulting people when they didn't speak French, and that he would order drinks for us so that I wouldn't have to

"Put up with their crap, mon ami."

The bar was jam packed with people, and was possibly the loudest saloon I'd ever been in.

We laughed and drank for hours. Henri would translate our conversation to the women and, occasionally, Dominique and I would share a few words in Spanish.

As Dominique and I bid adieu to our friends, Henri slipped me a joint. It was rolled and wrapped with a filter and looked very much like a Marlboro cigarette.

"Be careful, my friend," he cautioned.

I thought he meant don't get caught with that joint. I didn't realize that after a couple of hits in our room at the Sheraton I would be paralyzed for an hour or so. All I could do was lie there saying, "Henri!" and point to the cannabis, laughing like a maniac.

I was almost catatonic. My Spanish was gone; for that matter, most of the English I spoke was lost on me as well, missing somewhere in the delirious dither I was in.

I don't know how long it took for me to recompose, thirty minutes or an hour, but as the effects of the marijuana began to subside, I was finally able to pour some Champagne for Dominique and myself.

I spent the next night in Paris, which was a Sunday, at Dominique's apartment, watching an old Errol Flynn movie in English with French sub-titles.

Later, I called Michael in Los Angeles and he told me that the deal with the Iranians was about to go down and that I had better get back pretty soon so we could make the deal with the Shah.

It was difficult saying goodbye to Dominique. I was flying home in the morning, so when she dropped me off at the hotel, we almost couldn't let each other go.

Brad - CC McCartney - Brian Mitchell at Milwaukees Star 95

Brad Edwards
- San Bernardino -
KFXM

Dad teaches daughter
Cindi, golf.

Brad Edwards
- Hot 105 - Miami

Brad Edwards
Mc-s Door's concert
- K-men 5

Brad with XM Satellites Scott Walterman in Miami

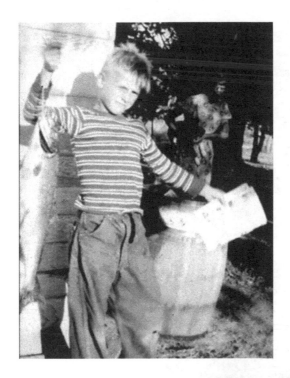

Claude catches Big
One in Oregon

Brad at KGBS

I-95 Morning Zoo -
Brad-Bill Taylor &
Lisa - Herb Sierra

Young Hooten in
US Air Force

Mindy & Malo - Miami

Chapter 28
Persia, Anyone?

Michael and I worked out the details of our contract with the National Iranian Radio and Television Network (NIRT) with Kamron Mashayekhi over the phone.

We put everything in storage and headed to Washington D.C., where Kamron was the bureau chief for NIRT. Too late, we'd find out he was also bureau chief for Savac, the dreaded Iranian secret police.

We met at the airport. He had the papers written up just like we had agreed, with the exception of the housing allowance. We had been told that if we wanted a two bedroom home to rent, with air conditioning and a phone, we'd be looking at about four or five thousand a month.

Kamron had only allowed for a thousand apiece. He said it was out of his hands, so Michael said, "Sorry, we'll have to go back to Los Angeles then, because it's going to cost a lot more than that to live there."

"Yes, but you will be compensated very nicely—a lot more than anyone else is earning in Tehran. Plus you will only be taxed at a rate of three percent," Mashayekhi said.

Michael was ready to walk, and so was I. That's what it took; Kamron finally grabbed the contracts, crossed out the old numbers, initialed them, and that was that. Within an hour, we would be on a Pan Am flight to London, the first step on our journey to Tehran.

We spent a day and night in London before moving on. Michael and I had gotten shit faced on the plane and needed the rest. We both shared that we didn't trust Masheyekhi and hoped that there was no basis for it.

I didn't realize how far Iran was from home. There were so many people on board, and with no smoking restrictions, there was an actual layer of smog that developed in the canopy of the 747. It was like being in Los Angeles on a smoggy day.

Welcome to Tehran, Yanks.

We landed at Mehrabad airport late in the afternoon, early in March. Tehran was surprisingly pretty. With an altitude of over 4000 feet, it's nestled at the base of the Alborz Mountains, about 150 miles south of the Caspian Sea resort of Chalus in the province of Mazandaran.

Chalus is a beautiful seaside resort, with lush forestry and plant growth that you won't see in other locations in Iran. It's where the locals went to get away. Tehran, on the other hand, was busy—a bustling metropolis.

Traffic is a continuous nightmare, especially since there appear to be no designated lanes. Cars, trucks, bicycles, and motor vehicles of every sort move in large, unorganized clusters. Every now and then, a traffic cop tries to reorganize the group a little, but rarely successfully.

Everyone honks their horns. Of all the busy cities I've visited in my lifetime, Tehran was the noisiest. The air was cool and the city was vibrant.

Our driver met us at the airport. Everywhere we went in Tehran, a driver accompanied us. This guy's job was to drive us to all official functions from the radio station, to work and back, and to pick us up and take us to the airport. He doubled as NIRT's spy. It was his job to snoop on our attitudes. That's just the way it was. No one trusted anyone, so someone had to keep track. We found out about our driver shortly after we met some of the other staff.

The first night at the Marmar Hotel was nice. Our room was okay, but the shower was very small. You had to raise one arm at a time to lather up, something most Iranians didn't worry about in the first place.

Our room had a standard, universal toilet. Outside the hotel, though, you had to poop in a little hole in the floor. It was disgusting, but, when in Rome....

Michael and I were quick to shower and head down to the International Bar at the hotel where a very interesting collection of human beings had gathered. Most of the guys were foreigners working for the Shah and living at the Marmar, so at the bar there were men from all over the world: Englishmen, Scots, Germans, Canadians, and Yankees, like Michael and myself.

We sat down and ordered a couple of beers, and the guy next to us laughed at almost everything we said. Finally, I turned to him and introduced myself as "Brad Edwards," and held out my hand. Michael did the same, and we met Stefano, a makeup artist of significant note in Europe.

Stefano was Italian and had done the make up for "Jesus Christ Superstar," which at that time had just been a big hit in the U.S. He had an incredible sense of humor. He was there working on a film project for the Shah.

Stefano was from Rome and was a genuinely friendly person—thin but handsome, with a broad smile and full of energy. Stefano, Michael, and myself hung together in Tehran for a while.

The National Iranian Radio and Television network was in a very large communications complex, nestled on the side of a large hill in Tehran. The offices and studios were an odd collection of poorly constructed rooms. Doors, for instance, did not have a system of conformity. There might be a door somewhere on the wall, but it did not have any relation to the door in the next room, either in size or structure.

I'd have to duck down to get through some doorways, and turn sideways to get through others. Some you could drive a truck through. The corridors going from floor to floor had no method either. There could be a few steps up where a room would be constructed, and then, moving on up the corridor, it might climb six or eight steps with another room at that level. Codes? What codes. It was fun to navigate, though. I got lost several times in the first week or so. It was a genuine adventure. I thought to myself, "No wonder so many people die when they have earthquakes."

The broadcast studio was unique as well. We had a German control board, Italian cartridge machines, and French turntables, all installed by Iranian engineers. It was functional, but getting each element on the air was tantamount to figuring out a Rubik's Cube.

For instance, to use the turntable, I had to disable one of the cartridge machines temporarily so that I could cue up the record. That meant that I had to make sure nothing was playing in the cartridge machine I was disabling, which we usually used to play some kind of a recorded promotion, like, "Serving Tehran, Isfahan, Tabriz, and the entire Persian Gulf. You're listening to the National Iranian Radio and

Television Network from Tehran on (Jingle) NNNNNNN - IIIIIII –
RRRRR – TTTTTTTTTT...."

If the cart machine was playing and I had to play the song, a lot of
the time I just put the needle on the LP and let it cue to the song while
I talked it up. All the while thanking my mentor, his majesty, Emperor
Bob Hudson.

Ted Anthony, from San Francisco, was our morning man. He
immersed himself into his show and the Iranian culture for about two
years and fell in love with and married an Iranian woman.

She was an exotic beauty; who could blame him. When Tehran
fell to the Ayatollah Khomeini, Ted was the last guy out and had to be
airlifted off the roof of NIRT and taken directly to a plane waiting at
Mehrabad Airport.

Ted would later resurface at the WWWW radio station in Detroit.
He told me later that the helicopter that came for him was almost shot
out of the sky during his escape.

John Colson and Frank Carpenter were two of the personalities
from Sheffield, England that had been hired two years before. Colson
was a cool, but younger Englishman that would follow directions when
told to. He was a blond-haired, blue-eyed kid of about twenty-four or
twenty-five, who was about five foot nine and thin.

He was well dressed, but had teeth that looked like a picket fence,
with a few of the slats kicked aside so that someone could sneak into
the yard. He immediately latched onto Michael and me because we
were big-market Yanks coming over to save the day.

Mashayekhi told us that they had made a mistake in hiring small-
market Englishmen to be their DJs. No one could relate to them
because they were so stiff. We had to be careful not to cross over the
line, which in an Islamic society is easy to do.

Frank, on the other hand, was as rigid as a corpse. We called him Ichabod, as in Ichabod Crane from *The Legend of Sleepy Hollow*. He was tall and gangly, with a large amount of hair on top of his head that he swiped aside, covering half his face. His neck stuck up from his shoulders and looked like it was at least twice as long as it was meant to be. When he spoke, his large Adam's apple bobbed up and down, and I couldn't help but stare.

It was Frank's job to show Michael the ropes at five o'clock, when the rock and roll show began. I pitied him, because Michael was one of the innovators of the rock format in America. Frank had been playing mellower rock previous to our arrival, but that was about to change.

My first day on the air went well. The people of Iran were not used to real, personable human beings chatting with them on the air.

I remember some of the songs I played on my debut that day: "So Into You" by The Atlanta Rhythm Section, "I Like Dreamin'" by Kenny Nolan, "You Make Me Feel Like Dancin'" by Leo Sayer, and tunes from Hall and Oates and other AC songs that the ladies liked in the late '70s. I loved them too, so it all worked out.

I got a call that first day on the air from a cute-sounding girl, who said, "I'm so excited about you being on the station. You sound so good." Then she asked if I'd play something for her by Cliff Richards.

"I love your voice. I hope you look as good as you sound," I told her. I didn't think she'd be too disappointed if we did meet, always keeping in mind the "sounds good, add fifty pounds" rule.

Her name was Sarah, her father worked for the Shah in an executive position and her two sisters were just back from the Sorbonne in Paris where they had gone to school.

I soon found out that this family was *very* close to the Shah, and that Sarah and her sisters were the Debutantes of Tehran.

When Michael hit the airwaves, his first set was cool, wrapping up with Peter Frampton's "Baby, I Love Your Way." It was so cool that Iranians were practically running out of their houses, pouring into the streets in jubilation.

Michael was a musical genius, and his pipes, which always maintained an extraordinary cool, blew everyone away. Frank practically pooped his pants. He thought Qu Mogadam, our program director, was going to come down there and behead someone.

Frank wanted Michael to lighten up on the music. Michael said not to worry about it and followed it with one mind blowing set after another. That night, people were waiting for Michael at the MarMar hotel. Two guys offered Michael some Hashish, which he declined, oh so reluctantly.

The desk clerk had a list of favorites he wanted Michael to play the next night. It was amazing, with that list of songs, by the way, was the clerk's gift of some hashish for Michael that he *did* except.

As it was, the hash coming in from Afghanistan was plentiful and potent. Michael couldn't wait until the next day so that he could go to the bizarre and buy a hash pipe.

I, on the other hand, was about to get my gift as well. Michael and I had scored fast and furious with the Iranians, and the people were ecstatic to have a radio station they could dig even though we were programming it for the English speaking faction working in Iran.

I told Michael and Stefano about Sarah and her sisters. They had described themselves thoroughly and I liked what I heard. I wasn't sure if I'd have to add fifty pounds this time because they were young and hip. I asked them to meet us in the lobby of the MarMar and said that we'd go out to dinner.

Michael and Stefano were excited, but nothing like when the girls walked into the lobby. They were pretty. Not beautiful, but pretty nevertheless.

Sarah was small and exotic. She had beautiful oval eyes that looked like she was a model for Thailand travel posters, not Pakistani as she said they were. She was wearing a full skirt that seemed to go well with the skin-tight pull over blouse she was wearing. Her skin looked tan, but it was a dark tan that made her green eyes stand out all the more. She fixated on me. I was reluctant because she appeared and later turned out to be only eighteen years old.

Her sisters, both nice looking, were taller, lighter skinned, and well cultured. Both were dressed in jeans and heels and had great happy faces. They all spoke English with a British accent. We got acquainted and, apparently, each of us passed the "Okay, you look good, so let's go to dinner" test.

Linda and Tamara were the older sister's names. I thought it was odd that they would all have American names, but we were off in what I believed to be some kind of Russian car that we could all fit into.

Sarah tried to manipulate herself next to me, but had to sit next to Stefano instead. As it turned out, we went to a Mexican restaurant; because we were in Tehran, Iran, it was quite a surprise.

It was also strange because we went to a building with only a few cars parked close by; the street was dark and there were no signs indicating that there was a restaurant anywhere near.

We walked into the foyer and there was a small neon sign that said, "Mexican Food." Then, there was a stairway going down to what appeared to be a dark basement. As we opened the door that didn't appear to lead anywhere, we found ourselves in a loud and very busy restaurant. Unbelievable. Where did all these people come from? It was fun and festive. There was just the right atmosphere for all of us to get acquainted. Sarah had finally muscled her way next to me and was very warm and friendly.

The restaurant was decorated very nicely in a Mexican motif, and they were playing Mexican music through the sound system, but the enchiladas I ordered bore no resemblance to any enchilada I had ever tasted. They were good though, I guess.

Michael and Stefano hit it off with the older sisters while I was swimming in Sarah's exotic beauty, and we all enjoyed the time. On the way back, the girls pointed out a park and said we should stop and play hide-and-seek.

Wow, that was different. So we played hide-and-seek. As soon as everyone took off, we realized that it was a ruse that the girls had concocted so we could pair off and do a little innocent kissing.

Sarah and I found ourselves on a ledge behind a very large bush. I gently turned her beautiful little face to mine and kissed her softly. Her response caught me totally by surprise. She wouldn't stop kissing. She wanted it deeper and deeper, and then I noticed she was rubbing her body against mine in an erotic gyration that got my attention.

I carefully put my hands up and under her full dress. She wasn't wearing any underwear. I was nervous though. We were in Iran. If I was caught, they would put me in jail for certain, but a hard-on knows no fear.

I pulled her dress up, turned and put her on the edge of the ledge, and softly took her. I had one eye closed and the other looking for anyone who might catch us.

I almost fell to the ground my legs were so weak. We had to snap out of it quickly, though, as we were joined in moments by the others, who never again mentioned hide-and-seek.

When we got back to the Marmar Hotel, I wanted to tell the guys what had happened, but didn't, even though the two of them suspected that I'd gotten lucky. Michael broke out his brand-new hash pipe, loaded it up with the stuff the desk clerk gave him, and off we went.

Michael would soon be in a new dimension. Getting him too stoned was nearly impossible. It would be like trying to bring down a water buffalo with a twenty-two rifle. It just isn't going to happen. You might make him stagger, but…

Chapter 29
Tehran Radio, and
"The Hits Keep Coming"

On the air at the radio station, I did what they called middays, from noon until 5:00 PM. It was a long shift, but we had a variety of interesting, odd, and sometimes surreal programs to break the monotony as we worked our way through the broadcast day.

We not only had a lot of Americans and Iranians listening, but also a variety of expatriates from all those countries we found nightly at the Marmar bar. For instance, to satisfy our German listeners, the noon hour started with five minutes of German news by a guy from Berlin who worked for Bell Helicopters in Tehran. His body odor was so bad that he stank to high heaven. It was a long five minutes.

He set up in the news studio across the glass from me and I gave him a hand cue to tell him when to start. When he was about through, he would hold up his left arm and slowly bring it down until, at the end of his newscast, he'd be pointing straight at me. It was almost like a seig heil salute.

It seemed like he put more work into timing out the end of his newscast than he did actually reading the news. He couldn't get one sentence out without stumbling all over himself. He'd look up, red with embarrassment, as if I knew he was screwing up. Hey, he was speaking German, what did I know?

Then, at the end of his newscast, I'd play a German hit song that he gave me—a lot of "Oom pa pa, oom pa pa" accordion music that the Germans like so much.

Then, at 1:00 PM, the news was read in Farsi (Persian), followed by a hit from Iran's Top 10. A lot of the time, their Top 10 included many of the same hits we played in the United States on a regular basis. Iranians were big fans of the U.S. and England. They loved our Western culture.

At 3:00 PM, a French woman read five minutes of news that was, of course, followed by a French hit. Those usually were pop tunes as well. I liked the French tunes, maybe because it kept Dominique alive in my mind. The French woman who read the news was no babe. She even had a large clump of underarm hair hanging down and out of her blouse sleeve, almost as if she was proud of it.

The real fun came at four thirty PM. There was ten minutes of Russian news, read by a very large, unpleasant-looking, "workers favorite" Russian woman. She reminded me of my Grandma Ruth.

She looked like she could kick the crap out of everyone in the building. I'd say, "hello," she'd nod, and then walk into the news booth. I threw her a hand cue, and off she'd go. She read fast, loud, and continuously, with no interruptions.

When she was through, she just stopped talking and walked away. It caught me off guard so completely the first time that, in my panic to get the record on, I knocked the needle across the LP, skipping across the cuts. All of it on the air.

After that, I'd watch her intently, trying to catch a clue as to when she would be coming to the end of her newscast, but she caught me off guard again and again. When she was through, she simply turned and left the studio.

I told Michael about it, and we had a good laugh, but nothing like the day he was in early and witnessed it for himself. When she came into the studio, she grabbed the water pitcher and just took a big swig right out of it, never minding the fact that there were three clean glasses right next to it.

She slammed it back down as if she had been in a chugging contest with a couple of frat brothers, looked at Michael and me, wiped her mouth with the back of her hand, and gave us a look that seemed to say, "Screw you, Yankee imperialistic dogs," and went into the news booth.

As her newscast was coming to a conclusion, I was once again caught unawares, as Michael and I were chatting. Crap, she was halfway out of the building by the time I collected myself and got a grip on the situation. I finally got the next record on the air. We were laughing so hard it hurt.

After a few weeks, the fun was just about over for us. They hounded us daily for our passports, saying that we wouldn't be paid until we gave them up, which was precisely what we didn't want to do. If they had our passports we'd be stuck in Iran for the duration of the contract.

We spoke with the director of NIRT, whom they said was the Shah's brother-in-law. He was an interesting man. He spoke perfect English and was educated in London, so he, too, spoke with a British accent. It seemed odd coming from the lips of this Iranian; he was charming, but brutally direct.

He told Michael and me that he had called us in to say we would not be getting the additional housing money that Kamron Mashayekhi had approved in Washington DC, because Kamron had no authority to do so.

We argued that the extra housing was part of our original bargain with him from the day we began our negotiations on the phone from Los Angeles. We told him it would make it difficult for us financially and that if we didn't get the allowance we might not be able to stay.

"You will stay, and you will take the pay we agreed on without the extra money," the director said. "Now get back to work, and I don't want to hear anymore of this," he sternly concluded.

Apparently, this is the kind of bullying that the Brits had been putting up with. All it did was piss Michael and me off. We had already discussed it and agreed that if something happened and the Iranian's screwed us out of anything, we'd bolt back to the States.

Chapter 30
The Great Escape

We had met a young mechanic from Canada who was working for Iran Air, who had a friend with the travel agency that handled all of the NIRT travel business. When Michael and I signed the contract with Mashayekhi in Washington, we insisted that we have round-trip tickets issued to us, but those could be yanked from us whenever the Iranians chose, unless we could create a diversion.

The travel agent turned out to be an Iranian woman who laughed when we told her we had round-trip tickets. Her name was Banda. She was short and wore tight jeans and small-heeled boots, like so many of the Iranian women of the day. She spoke in rapid bursts and seemed to laugh when she wasn't supposed too, like when we told her we had round-trip tickets back to Los Angeles and that if anything went wrong, we were gone.

"Ha ha, your tickets are worthless if the Shah's people decide to cancel them," she said. She had big round eyes that were more like olives than eyes, but attractive because of their uniqueness.

"Is there any way of trading these in for new ones?" I asked.

"Not without Mr. Mashayekhi knowing that they have been cancelled," she replied. "But I could change the routing on them, which might buy you a short time if you know when you might want to make your escape."

Escape. There it was. Escape. This was way before the computer age, so we thought we could buy *some* time.

That's the first time we had heard that word in connection with our wanting to leave. And that's what it was, because these guys had no intention of just letting us leave when we wanted. Every day they would demand our passports, saying, "You can't get paid until we have your passports."

Kamron Mashayekhi phoned us and wanted to chat about our little misunderstanding concerning the housing allowance.

"I didn't say I would make it right," he explained. "I said I'd try to make it right, but I was overridden."

His reply was halfway honest even though there was no doubt that he'd offered us the higher amount. We told him that we might have a problem with that, and he offered a veiled threat.

"Leaving Tehran could be complicated," he informed us. "Our courts take breach of contract very seriously."

He was telling all this to me on the phone. I looked up at Michael, who was giving me a puzzled, what-the-hell-is-he-saying look. So I told Kamron that we weren't thinking of leaving. We just wanted to take it a little higher to get some satisfaction. That's when Mashayekhi said, "I'll tell you what I can do. I can offer you free transportation on Iran

Air to any location we travel, for a week every six months. How does that sound, my friend?"

I looked at Michael, winked, and said, "That's pretty cool, Kamron. We just need to be able to cut some of our expenses, and that sounds like it may be the answer." I held up my right hand to Michael as if to say, "I'm jerking this guy's chain."

Mashayekhi had already made that offer while we were still in Washington D.C. and must have forgotten about it. I tried to sound a little overenthusiastic so he would think that we just wanted a concession and now we were happy. Mashayekhi was anything but a fool, though; he was sharp as a tack.

We were reasonably sure he bought it, because the next day Qu Mogadam came up to us all smiles and said, "I hearing all things are now okay, huh?"

Michael shook his hand and said, "Yeah, this is good for everyone. We'll get those passports to you right away."

We were only a few days away from some sort of Islamic Holiday, an occasion when all the NIRT broadcast managers would go up to their retreats on the Caspian Sea. Kamron was in Washington D.C. and Qu was headed for the Caspian, so we began plotting our escape.

We knew that, in the Iranians eyes, they had given us consideration, and that if we didn't do as they wanted, they could slam our butts in jail for breach of contract. Iranian jails are seriously bad news.

Any jail would be awful, but if you saw *Midnight Express*, a movie about an American caught smuggling dope out of Turkey who subsequently got thrown into their jail, well, multiply that ugliness by ten, and you've got an Iranian jail. The immediate precursor to getting you into prison is confiscation of your passport.

Giving up our passports would seal our fate. We'd be doomed. We wouldn't be able to travel, much less leave the country if we surrendered them, and they had been pressing hard for them on a daily basis. That fact was on our minds as we began making quiet arrangements to escape from Tehran.

We had to get with Banda at the travel agency and build up a ticket rerouting ruse in hopes of buying some time. She said that all we could hope for was putting them off for one day, maybe two, and that would be only if they weren't too concerned. It would take some time to sift through the paperwork.

As it turned out, we had other concerns. The first challenge was how to leave the hotel with our baggage and trunks, past the receptionist's ever-watchful eye, without raising any suspicion at five o'clock in the morning, which is the hour we planned to make our escape to the Mehrabad airport. We needed to leave then because Michael was slated to fill in for Ted Anthony on the morning show, as Ted and his Iranian wife were planning to head for their Caspian Sea getaway like all the others.

Ironically, we didn't feel we could trust Anthony with our plan, even though he was an American ex-patriot. We didn't know how deep his friendship with the Iranians went. After all, he did marry one of them. He might have been looking to score points with them; we didn't know.

First, we told Michael's driver that he'd take a cab to work because we were going to get up early and move our belongings to our new apartment. Banda thought of that.

She wrote down the address and directions to an apartment that she knew was for rent. She took the time to write out the directions from the Marmar in Persian (Farsi), as though we were going to give them to the cab driver.

Once we got to the clerk, the always-curious but suspicious Iranian dude at the front desk, we'd tell him our reason for leaving that early was to get over to our new apartment to drop off our belongings and, "oh, by the way, do you think the cab driver will understand these directions?"

At least that's how the plan was developing in our minds. If we pulled it off, there wouldn't be anyone awake to snitch us out.

Now, what to do about the morning show that Michael was supposed to do. If we just let the station go to dead air at 5:00 AM, someone would call Qu Mogadam up at the Caspian, and he'd start a chain of events that would probably land us in jail. That's when we decided to take John Colson into our confidence.

When we explained what our plan was, Colson felt like he was in a 007 plot.

"You Yanks have got balls the size of cantaloupes, you do." he exclaimed. "How can I help?"

"Okay, John, here's the plan," Michael explained. "Brad and I are going to leave the Marmar at 5:00 AM...." He went on to explain our hotel exit.

"What we need for you to do is fill in for me on the air. That way, no one will be suspicious," Michael said.

"So, Michael, what will I tell them we did, traded air shifts?" Colson queried.

"No no. Tell them I slept late, you heard the station go dark for a few minutes, so you raced into the station to get it on the air," Michael instructed. "Then, tell them after an hour or so that I called and said I had forgotten we were moving to our new apartment and would you mind taking the shift? That way they'll just think it was a miscue—an irresponsible one, but typical Yank crap, right?" Michael finished.

"I think that'll work, mate," Colson concluded.

It wasn't so much a plan as it was a scenario that made sense. It had to, because the Shah's boys would do whatever they had to in order to keep us there. Tomorrow was showtime.

The plan was finished. We were set to take off from Mehrabad Airport at 11:30 AM on a Pan Am flight headed directly for Frankfort, Germany. It was about a seven-hour flight. We told Colson that we'd *call him* when they called our flight, and then he could call Qu Mogadam to tell him that he had no idea where we were.

By the time Qu's men chased us down, we'd be in the air on our way back to the good old USA: Yankee freedom, the best in the world.

We called a cab and then dragged all our stuff, including two trunks full of what we thought we'd need for a couple of years in Tehran, down to the front desk.

Our buddy, Ali, was behind the desk.

"Going someplace?" he asked.

"Yeah, we're moving into our new apartment this morning,"
I responded.

"Well, the hotel hasn't been paid yet. What are you going to do about that," he asked.

We hadn't thought about that, but we both had been in a similar situation when a radio station owed a hotel for our first several weeks in town.

"Hey, you don't think the Shah would try to cheat you out of the money, do you?" I asked.

"Certainly not!" Ali exclaimed.

"Well then, would you be kind enough to ask the cab driver if he knows the way to this address?" Michael asked, handing him the directions to the empty apartment that Banda had drawn out for us.

He took the note and studied it for a minute, just to make sure it was legit.

"I know this place," he said. Then he called the cab driver over, and they mumbled back and forth for a minute, and then he said, "No problem. You go ahead, and we'll get in touch with NIRT (the radio station) and get payment through the proper channels."

I caught a glimpse of Michael's face, and I knew that he knew that I knew we were pulling it off. The cab driver began loading our belongings into his taxi.

We shook Ali's hand, thanked him for a great stay, and told him that we'd see him from time to time.

"Tehran had never heard these great radio programs of you two before," he said in parting. "We are liking it bery, bery much."

It made me think that we hadn't given him a fair chance; maybe he was okay after all. We waved as the taxi pulled away from the Marmar. Now, what is this cab driver going to do when we tell him to forget the directions and take us to the airport.

After a few blocks, I said, "Take us to Mehrabad airport." The cab driver threw one arm over the seat and looked back at me and said, "You are not wanting to go to theese place?" He held up the directions.

"No, just to Mehrabad airport, thank you."

"Okay," he said with a puzzled look on his face.

I knew Michael was thinking what I was thinking. Will this Iranian asshole turn us in to somebody? It seemed like they all had some sort of neighborhood network that they were collectively hooked into, like the Borg. Screw it, we had to keep going.

Mehrabad was crowded as usual. It was almost 6:00 AM by the time we got there. We lugged all our belongings up to the Pan Am ticket counter and shuffled our passports off to them for review.

Everything seemed to be in order, but then a guy in a suit called us over to the next counter. My heart sank. I thought we were caught, but it wasn't that. We were overweight. I almost laughed with relief.

Michael said, "Hey, the Shah paid for us to get here, I hope he'll pay for our return."

The guy looked us both over and said,

"I might have to make a call on that." Michael took a chance and slipped the guy a twenty dollar bill. He hesitated for just a second, looked around, and said, "I don't think there ees a problem, thank you bery much."

With that, he put all our stuff on the conveyor belt to purgatory. Phew! Now the longest wait of our lives.

Mehrabad airport, not unlike many other airports in that part of the world, had a variety of security personnel who were standing around with machine guns. In case of a coup, they had to secure all communications and the airport first. It seemed like the Shah had hired the ugliest and meanest looking sons of bitches to do his work. It was intimidating just being close to these guys.

Our flight was scheduled to pull away from the gate at 11:25 AM, but about an hour before, they called Pan Am flight 225 to Frankfort for boarding. It was early, but that was our flight and our cue; Michael called Colson and told him we were off.

"Tell those Iranian jaggoffs that we're two American's they won't get a chance to screw over again." Michael yelled into the phone. Colson said he was proud of what we were doing.

"Good luck, Yanks. God speed, and I'll call Qu Mo Gut Damn," which is what the Brits called him.

"Maybe we'll have a pint in London next time around, eh mates?"

We headed out to the tarmac for our flight, but things were not right. The flight they had called was leaving for Isfahan, a city south and inland from Tehran. Oh, God, they had called the wrong flight.

Now Qu's men will have time to track us down at the airport; the jig is up. The cat was out of the bag. Oh, man, what to do? Michael was right; we just had to wait it out. It was only another forty-five minutes to an hour, the longest minutes of our lives.

We both sat silently, knowing that a couple of Iranian goons would be there to grab us at any minute. Sure enough, after about half an hour, two Iranian special police, sporting machine guns, were coming over to us.

I nudged Michael with my elbow. He said, "Shit" under his breath. I knew we were screwed, but they just kept on walking past us. Whew! I almost passed out. False alarm.

Then, finally, after what seemed like an eternity, they called our flight, and we hurried on board. Within a few minutes we were in the air on that beautiful Pan Am 747 headed west by northwest.

Soon, the pilot was on the intercom saying that we had just left the Royal Republic of Iran, and that to the right of the aircraft was Istanbul, Turkey. Michael held his middle finger up to the porthole window and waved goodbye to the Shah.

We both gave each other a high five and ordered the first of what would be a long string of celebratory drinks on this flight.

Chapter 31
Phew! That Was Close

Traveling with the sun, we escaped Tehran at 11:30 in the morning and arrived at LAX in Los Angeles at 11:30 that night. With time changes and all, it amounted to something like twenty-one hours of flying.

The two of us were bone tired and very ragged when we finally got home. We stayed in a motel in Playa del Rey, close to the airport, our first night back. Just before our heads hit the pillow, Michael called his girlfriend and told her that we were back. She said the Iranians had already called her saying simply, "Where are they? We will find them, so tell us." God, they were like the gestapo.

How in the hell did they get her phone number? Or her name for that matter? Hey, it was scary. The next day, Michael called Claude Hall at *Billboard* magazine and told him how the Iranians had screwed us around.

Claude was angry on our behalf. He called Kamron Mashyekhi and told him to call off the dogs or he, Claude, would expose them for what they were doing to the talent who signed on with them. That was the last we heard from the Iranians.

I saw Mashyekhi on "60 Minutes" about a year or so later. Mike Wallace was questioning him about his activities as an agent for Savok, which was the Iranian secret police. He operated here in the United States using the cover of being the head of the National Iranian Radio and Television Network.

Chapter 32
Back in the USA

Within a few days, I was scouting for a new gig. I found one at a Heritage Top 40 station in San Jose, California, called KLIV. They had a staff of great people who had all been there for years and had developed close personal relationships with one another.

I was privileged to go in as their new swing man. That's the guy who does all the vacation relief, weekends, sick fill-in and so on. John McCloud was the program director and afternoon talent, and Bob Ray was on mornings, with his wife, Christine, as the midday man, so to speak.

Simultaneously, I had gotten an offer in San Francisco at KDIA. It was a very hip urban format, a lot like Jim Maddox's Majic format, which was sweeping the nation by then, and was a lot of fun. The station was located at the base of the Bay Bridge, with a panoramic view of the San Francisco Bay and Alcatraz.

I was the only white guy on the staff, and I was treated like a brother. I loved those guys. So now I was working for two stations, hoping I would be free when the other station needed me. I was making good money and having a ball.

It was a great summer, 1977, with a ton of memorable hits. The Bee Gees and disco were very hot. I was filling in for Bob Ray one morning and was doing some commercials after the shift when we got word that Elvis had died. I couldn't believe it.

Elvis was truly The King. I loved him. When I was in high school, I used to joke that he was like my big, hillbilly brother. Quickly, I put together a montage of songs and words and made a kind of tribute to The King.

It was just wrong that the King of Rock and Roll was dead. It didn't seem possible. He was so young, but Elvis's life had been a string of odd events for years. I was sorry I hadn't seen him in Las Vegas when RCA had offered me some free tickets a few years before.

Star Wars was still doing well in the theaters. My buddy Dick Edlund was the special effects creator on the film. I thought about how much he and I were missing by not sharing our thoughts as we did when we were kids.

The last time I saw Dick was at the Denny's on Santa Monica Blvd at the Hollywood freeway in 1969. Dick showed up with no less than three top-of-the-line 35 mm cameras hanging around his neck.

I told him I was working for Storer Broadcasting's KGBS, in Hollywood, but you know, I didn't think he believed me. I had told so many grandiose stories prior to getting into radio that I wondered if he believed me then.

I was desperate to be somebody—so much so, in fact, that there was a lot of b.s. on my resume. Fortunately for me, too many people saw through my crap, and it was too embarrassing for me to keep up the charade. Besides, when I found radio, I didn't have anything else to lie about. I loved the business so much and was proud to live with who I was, even though I wasn't somebody, yet.

Losing my friend Dick was a serious blow to me. It wasn't just my drinking and lying all the time; it was also because of the way I was living. I had no respect for others and was constantly cheating on my wife. Dick, Arlene, and I had been really good friends early on.

We would play cutthroat Pinochle most Monday nights. Dick was over for dinner very often, and he could see the erosion in our marriage caused by my drinking. He refused to go with me when I was drinking, in part to show his disdain for my behavior.

As I kept up my irresponsible lifestyle, I began losing most of my friends. They couldn't count on me. Eventually, I wouldn't let new friends come into my life because I knew I would let them down. My only friend was radio. I tried not to let it down.

One of the wonderful gifts of sobriety in an alcoholics program like mine is that you get to be "reborn" in many ways. It says in "The Book," to paraphrase: "A person rarely fails as long as he follows in our footsteps." Simple words of truth. One day I would reap those benefits, but not yet.

One evening I was filling in for the seven to midnight DJ on KLIV in San Jose. I had to clear some things up with my now ex-wife Arlene. I called her in Santa Monica, and we got into a heated discussion, which, by the way, is difficult at best when you're on the air. One minute you're screaming obscenities, and then it's, "Wait a minute, Arlene."

"KLIV and Brad Edwards, with Meco and the *Star Wars* theme and a chance for you to see the movie if you're the fifteenth caller right now at blah, blah, blah."

"Hold on a second, Arlene, let me get this winner's name."

"Hi, KLIV, you're caller number fifteen, and you are the winner. What's your name?"

Arlene waited patiently for me to finish. I started a record, and when I came back on the phone she was loaded for bear. She wanted a piece of my ass for whatever we were arguing about, and she let me have it.

"You inconsiderate son of a bitch, you have been screwing me on everything you promised," she said. "You are the world's biggest asshole, and you don't give a shit about anything I want," she continued. Arlene rarely cussed, so I knew she was really angry with me.

I noticed that all the phones were lighting up. We must have had at least ten lines coming into the station, and they were all lit. I put Arlene on hold and took a call.

"Hey, I don't know if you know it but some woman is on your radio station cussing up a storm," the caller said. That's when I noticed that our contest line, including the caller I was speaking to, was up and on the air.

So everything Arlene had been saying went on the air, but not my side of the conversation because my mic wasn't on. Good grief.

"We must be getting one side of someone's CB or something," I told my caller.

By 1977, I was making a major transition in my life. I had just gone through a harrowing experience in Iran, my ex-wife and children were in Los Angeles, and something was happening within me. I was separating from my previous years and moving on to the next plateau of my life.

It was scary and exciting at the same time. Al Stewart's song "Time Passages" was prophetic. I was finally letting go of Arlene, my decision-making process was a bit more mature, and I felt like I was in a new and better place mentally.

Chapter 33
Fool on the Hill

Within a few months, Scotty Brink, a friend of mine in Los Angeles who had worked for 93 KHJ Boss Radio, called me. He asked if I'd be interested in taking a program director's job in El Paso, Texas. He was consulting the station and remembered I was back.

It was a country station. I told him I had a very difficult time relating to country music, but he told me that El Paso was a very hip country market. He said that he'd fly me down to meet the GM, and we could decide after that. That did sound like fun; so I went.

Brink told me that the station was owned by a couple of guys in Houston, who also owned a construction company. They had bought it as an investment but didn't know what to do with it. The GM was a guy named Bob Gourley, who was a minister who had lost his job after having an affair with one of the women at the church. So they asked him to run it, and he needed some professional help.

Gourley met me at the El Paso Airport. He was dressed in a brown plaid suit with a pair of brown and white shoes, showing several inches of white sweat socks. His pants were high water, and overall, it was the screwiest ensemble I had ever seen.

Simultaneously, Gourley had taken the opportunity to fly in a chief engineer prospect he was hoping to hire that weekend as well. Randle Sather came in from Tacoma, Washington. He was the oddest-looking goofball I had ever seen. Sather was on the same plane I was on, and somehow I hadn't even noticed him.

He was big, heavy, and tall, with a full beard. He wore large, square glasses and seemed as though he was in orbit around reality, but couldn't reenter. Sather was very different, but he fit what we were putting together for the station. So the three of us headed out to the good reverend's car, which was an AMC Eagle that always looked like it was going uphill.

As we drove along, Gourley said, "Oh, by the way, Scotty said that we should fire this up." He pulled out a joint. Good grief! I looked back and Sather's face looked like he'd just seen a ghost.

Before I could digest what was going on, he had it lit, took a hit, and passed it on to me, saying, "'Ear!" Within minutes, the three of us were rolling along I-10 headed west from the airport and were having an out of body experience. As I would find out soon enough, Gourley never smoked anything that didn't just tear the top of your head off. He would later say it was for health considerations. Why have to take several tokes on a harsh joint when you can get the job done with just a couple of hits.

I was hanging on with both hands, trying to maintain. We were passing downtown El Paso at that moment and Gourley pointed out where El Paso ended and Juarez began. It had been just one big city many years ago, called El Paso del Norte.

As it turned out, he loved playing the minister ruse. Later, I enjoyed being his stooge when he would foist the game on unsuspecting visitors from time to time. He had me, hook, line and sinker, until he broke out the joint. Even then I wasn't sure. "No wonder he lost his job with the church," I thought.

Then, nah, he can't be a minister. Finally, he told us he was just screwing with us. We laughed, pretty much the whole rest of that weekend. I was hoping my interview went well, because working for Gourley would be fabulous.

Finally, after what seemed like a drive across the entire state of Texas, we arrived at Gourley's home. He hopped out, and I poured myself out, all the while wondering if my legs would respond. We practically had to put smelling salts under Sather's nose to snap him out of it.

That's how Gourley liked it. It was fun first, and then we would work as hard as we played. He lived by that rule, so we had a lot of respect for one other because we both did a lot of each.

Sather and I spent most of the first day completely trashed in Gourley's living room, trying to figure out important things like what the heck Tom Waits was trying to express on his album, "Nighthawks at the Diner," which was one of Gourley's favorites.

After a few days of great fun, Gourley told me that he wanted me to be his number one and that I could hire the rest of the staff, except that he'd like for me to consider keeping the morning man on the station, John Allen Weitz.

I would find out that John Allen Weitz was an incredible talent. He was one of the most gifted radio personalities I would ever hear, and he was a great guy to boot.

Gourley and I had agreed on a salary and some basic programming thoughts, clinching the deal at a bar called The Kentucky Bar in Juarez, Mexico, across the Rio Grande. We both agreed that Sather would make a good chief engineer, so he'd be headed for Texas as well.

Chapter 34
Let the Party Begin

I rented a beautiful condo that was "High on a Hill Overlooking El Paso," or so the song goes. My view included the cities of El Paso and Juarez, Mexico. Juarez was a wonderful place for a drinker. I was able to completely stock my bar for about fifty dollars. Vodka, Tequila, Bourbon, Scotch, you name it. It all sold for a little over two bucks a fifth.

Carta Blanca beer was something ridiculous like $3.50 a case. We'd go shopping at one of the biggest Super Mercado's in Juarez where they had big pints of iced-down Carta Blanca beer to drink while you shopped, for eleven cents each. Just throw the empties in the shopping cart and they'll add 'em up. Many times I'd head back across the bridge with a king-sized buzz on. Oddly, the best Chinese Restaurant in El Paso was in Juarez, the Shangri-La.

I was about to settle in to several years of great fun and drunken adventures. K102 was an off-the-wall progressive country station with no direction or design. No game plan, no fun, and, worse than anything, no revenue coming in. The on-air talent was awful, with the exception of John Allen Weitz. They had no core artists, Kinky Friedman notwithstanding. I felt the station needed to go to mainstream country to compete with the Heritage station, appropriately called KHEY. They owned the dial, but were complacent. Their music was all over the place, and their disc jockeys couldn't stop talking.

I had a small budget and very little talent to work with, but I took the job anyway. I hired every misfit outlaw DJ in town. All the guys who'd lost their gigs because they weren't going to put up with anybody's crap. All the rebels. The first among them that I brought in was Gary Keener, who had initially moved to El Paso just to be on XRock, a 150,000-watt monster broadcasting out of Juarez.

Gary Keener was the most negative individual in the world. Off the air he bitched and moaned about everything and everyone. Then, on went the mic, and he was the most positive, feel-good DJ I ever worked with. He had a great voice and he was good looking too—some of the major ingredients I was looking for in a DJ.

I disagreed with others who thought that DJ's looks weren't important. If you not only sounded good, but looked good too, fans were more inclined to listen and give you good ratings. Invariably, more listeners would show up at remotes if they knew that the DJ broadcasting was a looker.

I had a lot of respect for the other Gary on our team, Gary Perkins, God rest his soul. "Perk" was major league and wanted to come home to El Paso. He rarely hit the airwaves until he had polished off at least a six-pack, but no one ever knew it. Be it two beers or fifty, he was the same. He was never sloppy, and never nasty, just good. Perkins came home from San Diego where he had been at KSON for several years. He brought his bookkeeper girlfriend, Barbara, with him. We were able to put her to work in the front office.

The big chance I took was bringing in my friend Harry Osibin. I met Harry when I was in San Francisco. He had two loves: baseball and country music. Harry was a very metropolitan guy, very San Francisco. I went to Gourley and told him I wanted to take a chance on a talent. Some country people have their thoughts about whom they want and don't want on the air.

I told Gourley that Harry knew more about country music than all of us put together and that I thought he'd be great for the seven-to-midnight slot. Gourley agreed, and El Paso had their first Black DJ.

"Harry O" was a smash hit with El Pasoans. He was great on the air and, furthering his love of baseball, he organized the first K102 Baseball team and loaded it up with the biggest and best soldiers (ringers) he could find out at Fort Bliss.

One of our teammates on the K102 baseball team was a guy named "Moose." Moose was an Abram's Tank commander and was so powerful that almost every single time he came up to bat, they either walked him or he hit a home run. He was a phenomenal talent and a wonderful example of the quality of man we had soldiering for us.

Harry O himself was so accepted by El Paso that he was constantly signing autographs. It was a beautiful thing, and I miss my old friend. I miss him because I lost his friendship as a result of my drinking. It happened in St. Louis; I'll tell you about that later.

Hiring unique individuals was a trick I learned from Roy Schwartz at KGBS when he hired Emperor Bob Hudson and the others. If you can find the guys who sound great but can't keep their jobs because of egos or drinking or whatever and can somehow get their respect and attention, you'll make a lot of noise very quickly.

I'd have everyone over to my house almost every night, drinking and smoking dope and talking about how we were going to kick the crap out of the competition. They were great sessions, and that's what we did too. We kicked KHEY like a mule. Our guys were hip and slick. It took a couple of ratings books to hand them their hat, but we did, and it was fun.

By the end of that first summer in El Paso, I was in love with the city. The cicada's buzzed incessantly; it was warm to hot, but the skies were clear and the evenings cooled down nicely. It was fun to sit outdoors and enjoy the climate. The people of El Paso were warm and friendly, and the women were extremely beautiful—a combination of Texan and Mexican charm that can't be compared to anywhere else I've been in the world.

This collection of individuals whom I had the opportunity to work with proved most rewarding. John Allan would become and still is a great friend of mine. He was very clever, and one of the most creative individuals on the radio. He was also lightening fast with callers. We were lucky to have him.

Weitz did a bit most mornings called, "Mr. Kiss and Tell." Listeners would give him some inside information about something going on at a local company about such and such, and John Allen would look into it and then broadcast his version.

"Beep, beep, beep, beep. Mr. Kiss and Tell here with the latest scoop on who's being fired today at Justin Boots." He did it like Walter Winchell of yesteryear radio, and our audience loved it.

One of the sales guys at K102 was Andy Whatley. He was a great salesman with a wonderful personality. He recommended a young DJ he knew in Salinas, California with a ton of potential. His name was John Carrillo.

"Carrillo," he said, "is completely off the wall, but needs direction."

I gave him a call. Carrillo told me he'd been on the air at KTOM in Salinas for about a year and would love to fly to El Paso to interview for the gig. I was hoping he was as good as the hype, because I could really use a good overnight man, especially a Hispanic, since this was El Paso.

Gourley and I met him at the El Paso airport, and as Gourley liked to do, he played the "Minister who somehow got hold of a radio station" role again, and wore that damned plaid suit he thought was so cool.

Prior to Carrillo's arrival, I set him up, telling him Gourley was our GM and that he'd left the ministry to run the radio station that a couple of guys in the church owned and had turned over to him. As we were driving, Gourley pulled out a special joint for the occasion. As usual, this pot was the kind that you might not come back from, the kind that ripped you well past the sixth dimension.

When I lit it, took a hit, and passed it back to Carrillo, he looked puzzled as if we shouldn't be doing this in front of the Good Reverend. I said, "Pastor Gourley likes a hit or two every now and then." I could hardly keep from laughing, but Carrillo obediently took the joint, pulled a sizeable hit for himself, and then passed it back.

As we drove along, taking in the beautiful views of El Paso, the mountains, and the Rio Grande, I could see Carrillo's eyes begin to glaze over and knew that he was one hit away from tilt. Gourley drove straight to his home, close to the University of Texas El Paso.

When we pulled into Gourley's driveway, I didn't know if Carrillo was still with us. I held up four fingers, and he looked at my hand and said, "Thursday." We went inside and got to know one another.

Later, we went down to the Hacienda Restaurant. What a great place. Old-timers claim it had been the Fort Bliss Hospital during the Mexican American War back in the mid 1840s, and had been rebuilt a couple of times before someone bought the building in the 1920s and turned it into a restaurant.

It sat right on the U.S. side of the Rio Grande. Outside the window next to our booth, the mighty Rio Grande flowed so close you could almost reach out scoop some up in your hand. The Chili Colorado at the Hacienda was unbelievably tasty. Hot too, but when you stuffed one of their homemade flour tortillas into it and chased it down with a cold beer, it was a beautiful experience.

Carrillo, whose mother, Del, made some of the best homemade Mexican food in the world, was knocked out. He couldn't eat enough of their tacos and enchiladas, and I wasn't sure they'd have enough for that hungry boy.

After dinner, Gourley dropped us off and I called Sather and Keener and asked them to join Carrillo and me in Juarez. I wanted them to help me paint a picture of harmony and fun so that Carrillo wouldn't say no.

The four of us headed for Juarez to put together our deal at the Kentucky Bar, the same bar where Gourley, Sather, and I made ours. I thought it would be a good idea to get loose and have a little fun and close our contract the same way.

The Kentucky Bar was like a scene straight out of the Old West. The bar itself was brought in around the turn of the century and was purported to have been a favorite watering hole of the infamous Dallas Stoudemire, a U.S. Marshall the city of El Paso hired to clean up their town back in the Wild West days.

He had a rough reputation, and was known to shoot first and ask questions later. The bar was massive mahogany, said to have cost over a quarter of a million dollars when imported from Kentucky.

It was gaudy, but unique, including the meticulously laid tile trough that ran the length of the bar past patrons' feet as they drank.

"In the old days, there was no need to go to the men's room to take a leak. You just pissed in the trough," Ernesto, the bartender, said. Rare was the night that they didn't have to stop someone from using the trough. "More trouble than it's worth," he said. Beers were a quarter and a shot of Tequila was fifteen cents. I got to know Ernesto really well over the years.

Keener, Sather, Carrillo, and I were having a great time until about the seventh beer and I lost count of the shots of tequila. I said something Keener didn't like and he reached across the table and slapped my hat off. Well, I stood up very quickly and pushed him and his chair backward, dumping him onto the floor. Carrillo's eyes showed a look of horror on his face.

Every Mexican cop in the world seemed to be there in seconds and dragged our drunken butts down to the local hoosegow. I remember thinking, "This can't be good." What a great start. "Carrillo probably can't wait to get the hell out of El Paso and away from us screwballs."

The judge let us out after about an hour. Amazing how our fine turned out to be exactly what we had in our pockets. It was good justice though, because the Mexicans didn't put up with hotheads who couldn't hold their booze. Ironically, that hassle, with each of us getting in one good lick, bonded our friendship and gave me a reputation as a gunslinger.

The guys who worked for me took direction very well, and tried to stay out of my reach. Funny, actually, that was the only time anything like that ever happened, and Keener really took a liking to me. It was mutual. What about Carrillo? He shrugged his shoulders.

The next day, I took Carrillo down to the radio station. Sharon Hodge was on the air and I introduced her to him.

Sharon, by the way, would later marry Randle "Tex" Cobb, the heavyweight boxer. She was one of the most gifted talents in town, but at this moment, I told her to take the rest of her shift off because Carrillo was going to do a couple of hours to see how he liked it. When

I said that, he had a look of horror on his face because I hadn't shared my plans.

Sharon wished him good luck and left and I gave him a quick tutorial about the control board and told him I'd be in my office listening.

Carrillo freaked. His claim of on air experience was just as I suspected—b.s. He knew a little, so I just let him screw up until he started catching on. I ducked in and told him I ran down to the store and missed his first few sets, which by the way, were awful. He was so lost, but I sensed that he would prevail. Sure enough, after a few hours he began getting comfortable and some of his personality started bleeding through.

When he was relieved at 3:00 PM, Carrillo came into my office and asked, "Did I make it?" I looked at him and replied, "How soon can you get back to start work?" He jumped up and down like a little kid, and that began our friendship that has lasted for years.

Later Carrillo would tell me that when he went home to Salinas to pack up his stuff, he didn't even mention the fight at the Kentucky bar, lest he be talked out of coming to El Paso to work with this bunch of whackos.

Chapter 35
Hello, Mr. Leonard

Carrillo turned out to be like a little brother to me, and I still love him like that. I tried to get him hired wherever my career took me, because I knew he was a great talent, and that wherever he worked, the quality of the station was enhanced.

One thing that elevated Carrillo, who would later change his air name to John Rio, was a character that he and I developed called Mr. Leonard. Mr. Leonard was a fun-filled con artist that was always shucking and jiving everyone. He would call in from various locations with some sort of scenario that always sounded great on the radio, but which ultimately benefited Mr. Leonard.

Before long, his Mr. Leonard persona was earning him over a million dollars a year after he worked with Scott Shannon in New York City, and John Lander in Houston.

Meanwhile, back in El Paso.

One summer, we hosted the El Paso Rodeo from the fairgrounds. To get there, you took I-25 South, and then exited at Paisano Road going east. If you miss Paisano Road, though, your next stop is Mexico. It was a major hassle, because you then have to take the bridge across the Rio Grande, over to Juarez on the Mexican side, turn around, come back through customs, and then finally return to the U.S. I went over that scenario with Carrillo, telling him, "Be sure to take the Paisano off-ramp."

In the haze of multiple hits off his bong at the house, all that information was lost on our friend from Salinas.

When Carrillo finally got to the rodeo, he was an hour late. Here's how he explained his tardiness:

"I was headed south on Paisano, I thought, but I was so stoned that I thought I spaced it and got on I-25 Northbound, so when I saw Paisano, I knew I needed to go past it and get back on I-25 South, but I thought, no, wait."

Carrillo was very stoned.

"I would have to be going south on I-25 if I saw the Paisano off-ramp. That's when I saw the Mexican border. Man, I was ripped, but I had to cross over the bridge, turn around, and come back. I argued I was coming south looking for Paisano Street and accidentally kept coming south and went into Mexico by accident."

Every red flag at the border must have gone off. Carrillo looked and sounded like the profile of someone guilty of something, not to mention the fact that the customs agent probably couldn't see any pupils in his eyes.

"Pull into stall number three," the agent had said.

"No, no, see, I got here by accident, and," Carrillo had insisted.

"Stall number three, now!" the border guard had ordered.

"I just about pissed my pants," Carrillo said, "because I knew I had a couple of roaches in my ashtray."

After he had pulled into stall number three, Carrillo said,

"Flashes of *Midnight Express* went racing through my head, especially when they brought out the drug-sniffing dog."

The Customs officer had said, "Step out of the vehicle please, sir." When Carrillo did, the dog jumped in and went crazy. Naturally, there was clear evidence that Carrillo had been smoking dope, as the dog went nuts over the ashtray.

Then, Carrillo said, the dog had jumped in the back seat and begun digging his paws into the back of it. They pulled out the back seat, but didn't find any dope.

"It's probably in the trunk," the officer had said.

Once again, Carrillo said, he had thought he was surely going to piss his pants, because when they opened the trunk, the dog went nuts. Visions of a bag of dope long since forgotten, or God knows what else might have been in there raced through his mind. Meanwhile, the dog had been pawing furiously at the spare tire.

They had removed the spare, and there it was: a couple of marijuana seeds.

"They handcuffed me on the spot," Carrillo told us, "and ran me into the office and grilled me like a steak. I admitted that I smoked a joint earlier, but that I didn't have any more of the stuff."

Sure that he was going to spend the rest of his youth in prison, Carrillo spilled every bean in his bowl.

Fortunately for Carrillo, it wasn't a serious infraction, and the customs agents had just wanted to scare the crap out of him: mission accomplished. They had told him that they were going to arrest him for smuggling, as the amount in his ashtray was enough for a case, and the seeds in the trunk indicated that he'd been transporting the dope.

Then suddenly, the good cop had come in and had told Carrillo that if he even saw him at the border again, he'd run his ass in.

"Now get the hell out of here," he'd instructed.

Phew! Close call. They'd let him go this time.

Chapter 36
It Can't Last Forever

After a couple of years of great radio success, life changed a bit. Gourley bought his own radio station and left to run it. He asked me to set up the programming for him. I sure would miss that guy. Gourley was the best. By now John Alan Weitz, our morning talent on K102, had taken off for a job in Houston, so I was now doing mornings on the station.

Every day, I'd head over to the Gas Station, a very hip bar close to the University of Texas, El Paso, not far from the Sun Bowl. It appears I was drawn to bars with the word "Gas" in the title. This place was designed like an old gas station, complete with a couple of antique pumps out front.

Somehow, most days, I'd make it home and wake up at five AM, hit the button on the coffee maker, and then climb in the shower. Oh, how my head ached. I kept a joint in an extra soap dish and would light that thing up every morning just to take away some of the pain. After

I downed a cup of Java, I'd head down the hill to the station, my head buzzing and humming, to start another day.

Bonnie Davidson replaced Gourley. I thought that it was cool and progressive to hire a female GM. She looked like a housewife wearing a business suit. She appeared to be trying to look the part, but was having difficulty with what to wear. She was somewhat frumpy, with brown hair and eyes, but she did have a great smile. Not that she ever aimed any of them at me, amazingly.

My reputation was beginning to catch up with me. She knew of my drinking and womanizing ways and didn't like it, and told everyone who would listen that she didn't like it. Her first mission was to blow me out.

Apparently, she had made a deal with the owners in Houston that she'd manage the station, but she wanted to fire me. In that meeting, Gourley told her it would be her first mistake, and that I was about to take the radio station to the top in the next rating.

Gourley was a big fan, but he also knew that I was becoming a liability, so he suggested to her that if she'd work with me through the next rating period, she could fire me if the ratings didn't increase. If they went up, she could either stay on and work with me, or leave. She agreed.

Man, she hated me. It was all she could do to even talk to me. In spite of that, I knew that we had a great radio station and she did too. I was single and clearly helped myself to the ladies of West Texas, and it just gnawed at her. I could see the contempt for me in her eyes.

The kicker that took Bonnie over the edge was when one of the women working for us decided that she wanted a piece of me. She was married, and very straight laced, but she came after me with delight. She was a simple woman, not too attractive, but she had a nice body.

One day, out of nowhere, she came into my office, closed the door behind herself, and asked me if I'd make love to her. I was completely caught off guard. She and I were the only two at the radio station. So, in keeping with my policy of never saying no, I locked the door and bent her over my desk.

So, soon after that first encounter, which seemed to blow her mind, she began asking me to meet her at my place for lunch and to "show me some more things."

Fishing in those waters was not bright, or right. Even though she initiated it, I thought less of myself for partaking, as, apparently, I knew no boundaries. Had she'd been any homelier, I would have said no. I needed some demilitarized, no-penis zone that needed to be respected. She was married and very religious. She almost demanded that I take her home and

"Screw me good."

She would say things that would get her hot and fired up. Whispering, "Why don't you screw me in your office, right now?" It made me nervous, because she was taking chances that I knew would eventually get us both caught.

Then, she would sneak out late at night, after everyone had gone to bed at her house, to come over for a quickie. Of course the inevitable finally happened. One night she came over and I was already with someone. She was incensed. In her mind, I was cheating on *her*.

Almost immediately, she decided that she had sinned way too much to keep it a secret anymore. So, she went to Bonnie the GM and told her all about it. She admitted she instigated "some" of it, but Bonnie already knew I was the devil incarnate and had to be held responsible.

For Bonnie, this was the last straw. She went to the owners and told them, "One of us has to go." That's the day Bonnie lost her job.

Chapter 37
Are We Having Fun Yet?

Finally, K102 was sold to a broadcast group from Louisville, Kentucky, and Lee Masters was headed down to run the station. Lee had worked for Bob Pittman at WNBC in New York City. Pittman was the program director there, and was also behind MTV and AOL.

Lee was a party guy, but his programming philosophy was all about flip cards. "Only let the jocks say what is on the cards," he'd say. Lee was good to me, but I knew that my days were numbered. The religious group on our AM station must have begged for the opportunity to fire the Devil and his accomplice.

The so-called interim GM was one of the guys from our all-religion KISO, and he *got* to fire me. He was shaking in his boots as he told Carrillo and me that he had to let us go. Carrillo was an emotional young man, and cried. I just smiled and stared at him. I noticed that he kept a safe distance from me. Maybe he had heard about the fistfight I had had with Keener at the Kentucky Bar.

KHEY had been the big country gun in the market until my misfits and I knocked 'em on their butts. So, when Lee Masters let the GM of the religious station fire me and John Carrillo, it was gratifying that KHEY hired me immediately to do afternoons and to help clean up their music rotation.

I called my old friend Jhani Kaye at KINT 98, the big Top 40 station in the market, and urged him to hire Carrillo, telling Jhani what a great talent he was. Jhani put Carrillo right on the air, and he changed his name to John Rio.

KHEY, which was K102's competition, was a great station run by Jim Phillips, a Texas boy of the highest caliber. He gave me a lot of latitude. He knew his music was all wrong, and he had me straighten it out. Phillips was smart because when he hired me, he asked what I thought was his weakness. I told him it was the music. We went right back to number one in El Paso's next rating, knocking off K102 and Lee Master's flip card readers.

In the short time I spent at KHEY, I got to know Dick "Buck" Buchannon, who did seven 'til midnight on KHEY. Dick was a great guy who just loved life, and he and I decided to share an apartment high up, overlooking the city.

It turned out to be one of the best situations for both of us. We were both clean freaks. We had a beautiful place and kept it that way. Buck liked the ladies too, so between us, women were dropping in day and night. To top it off, Buck was a great cook. Being a New Mexico boy, he could do things with a jalapeno that I didn't know were possible, or even legal.

I was unfulfilled though. I came to the realization that I was in El Paso, Texas going sideways and that I needed to get back on course with my career. That's when my old friend Harry O called from St. Louis again and asked me to do mornings on Majic 108. Buck was a great guy. When I told him I had to head for St. Louis, we were both bummed. I still miss Buck. He is one of my few friends I didn't lose because of drinking.

As it turned out, St Louis didn't work for me. It was a great place with super people, but the vibe was way off. My friend Harry O was working his first management position and wasn't getting any help from his boss, my old Majic friend Jim Maddox, either. The complexity of the format on Majic 108 was so tedious that my alcoholic brain was about to explode.

After work one day, Harry O, Carrillo (now John Rio), and I met over at the San Louisan for drinks. God knows how many beers and shots of tequila it took, but I told Harry that he didn't have a clue, and that he ought to quit. As you might imagine, he didn't take it well. Later, I tried desperately to take it back, to no avail.

Some will say that the hurtful things an alcoholic says when he's drunk and in a blackout are how he really feels. Nonsense! Most often, we're throwing out thoughts to evoke a reaction, many times saying just the opposite of what our real thoughts were. I didn't mean a lot of the things I said when I was drunk.

It cost me our friendship. It still saddens me, as Harry was a fabulous guy. It's just that at that point, I had no patience left and the symptoms of drinking had left me flying off the handle often.

Except for Nancy, one of our sales executives, I found nothing to like in Saint Louis. The radio station was located in and old dilapidated building with a UHF TV station. We were tucked in one corner of the building with the control room window showing a view of a few disgusting old smoke stacks and dilapidated buildings thrown in, close to downtown, in an industrial section of the city.

Nancy was a Missouri girl and was a tremendous sales person. She was about five foot five, with sandy blonde hair, beautiful eyes, and a body that would make birds chirp in an old painting.

Nancy felt compelled to come over to the Saint Louisan Hotel, where they put me up for a couple of weeks, and take me off on a get-acquainted tour of the city, ending up at Laclede's Landing.

Laclede's Landing was established as a trading post in 1764 by French fur trapper Pierre Laclede on the Mississippi River. They were just wrapping up a complete makeover, and it was a fabulous site on the mighty Mississippi. When we went back to the hotel, I asked her up for a drink, which began a romance that lasted months.

We might have had something long lasting and special if, after only a few months, I hadn't done the same thing with one of the other ladies, who was also on the sales staff and couldn't wait to tell Nancy about it. Nancy rarely spoke to me again. It actually hurt, a lot. I was beginning to feel something inside me. I don't know why I thought it wouldn't hurt Nancy's feelings. I was a jerk again.

I didn't like Missouri that much, not because of the people or location, but more because of myself, and the way that I was handling my life. I was beginning to realize that I wasn't a kid anymore, and that if I wanted any success in life, personally and professionally, I'd better do something about it, now.

For openers, I promised our GM Barry Baker that I would not drink for the rest of my time there—about five months. John (Carrillo) Rio and I shared an apartment from February to May of 1980. Rio did the all-night show and I did mornings. When I got off, we'd smoke dope, play backgammon, and eat thousands of White Castle burgers.

I kept my promise to Baker, and when our deal ended in late May of 1980, Saint Louis was in my rearview mirror. I was headed for El Paso to spend some time with friends. Then I'd take off for Costa Rica, where I had a chance to work for an English-speaking radio station there.

Chapter 38
Costa Rica

I packed up for Texas, figuring it to be about a five joint trip. I wished my good friend John Rio good luck and headed out the door. I hadn't had a drink in months, and I was dying for one, but I waited until I hit Memphis, where I turned right and started across Arkansas toward my beloved El Paso.

I pulled into a convenience store just on the Arkansas side of the state line and bought two Tall Boy cans of beer: yum, yum. They were tall and cold, and I was back out on the road for some good old drinking and driving.

After a couple of miles, I fired up a joint and got a good buzz on, and then I reached down and grabbed myself a can of the nectar of the Gods. I pulled that bad boy up to my lips and drank half of it down, feeling the cool, wonderful taste of the beer crossing over everything sensitive in my mouth and throat, on it's one-way trip to my stomach.

Ah, what a great feeling. Within seconds, I felt the additional rush break its way through to my brain. Finally, I was back in my most comfortable state. I reached down and grabbed the joint out of the ash tray and lit it back up, taking a couple of monster hits off it.

When I looked up, to my left and beside me was an Arkansas State Trooper. I just about shit my pants. He wasn't looking. I let the smoke out slowly and just kept it on track. "Oh my God, am I speeding," I wondered. "Am I staying within the lines?"

I panicked a bit, but I soon relaxed when the trooper took the next exit. Phew! I cursed the trooper for momentarily stealing my rush.

After visiting with some friends in El Paso and getting knocked on my ass by more of that cheap Tequila at the Kentucky Bar, I caught a flight to Mazatlan, which was the first leg on my journey to San Jose, Costa Rica.

Friends had told me about a company looking for American radio talent to work for them on their English-speaking station. I spoke with somebody who was apparently the first contact to touch base with before coming to Costa Rica and told him, "I'm coming anyway, so if you have something, fine. If not, that's okay too."

I knew that if I showed up in San Jose, Costa Rica, they'd have to put me on the air. If they didn't, screw 'em. I wanted some me time.

I spent a couple of drunken days in Mazatlan, days I still can't remember, and then headed for Mexico City. While I was in line to get my boarding pass for the flight to San Jose, there was a guy at the reservation desk having it out with the agents.

He was yelling and screaming about getting his ID, passport, and paperwork stolen from him, and the fact that he'd gone over all this with them the day before. He said, "Didn't the U.S. Consulate's office clear everything up?" He was loud and out of patience, but he finally got through and was given his boarding pass.

He was a very hip and good-looking young Hispanic guy, about my age, who spoke perfect English, with no accent. Finally, he quieted down and picked up his bags and ticket and moved on. When we boarded the Mexicana Jet to San Jose, he was my seat partner. He told me that three days earlier he had spent the night on the beach in Mazatlan and had had everything stolen from him. I thanked my stars that that hadn't happened to me as well, because I did the same thing several times over the years. He had no ID and had come to Mexico City because his journey was special.

He was the twenty-second child born to a woman in San Jose, Costa Rica, and he was the only one adopted out. After all these years, she was dying of cancer and she wanted to see the only baby she let get away. He had been invited to come and join the family to celebrate her life and to meet his many brothers and sisters.

Having no ID was a big snag, and the Mexican's wouldn't let him pass until the U.S. consulate cleared things up for them. His name was Michael, and he told me that they had finally accepted his paperwork and that that chapter was closed. He said that the past few days had been a nightmare. Michael was a ski instructor in Utah; he had lived a privileged life, as a very wealthy American couple had adopted him. He said that a lot of his relatives would be waiting for him at the airport.

As we deplaned, Michael was in front of me and the cameras were rolling. Lights, cameras, and applause: Michael's story was all the news in San Jose. The twenty-second child of a dying Costa Rican mother whose last wish was to see the only child she gave away, front page? You bet.

Michael asked me along for all the festivities of the reunion, but I declined, knowing that his family would want him all for themselves.

At the top of the list of traits we shared was our mutual enjoyment of a cold beer, or ten—beers and tequila.

One evening after his reunion, we were in the bar at the Irazu Hotel, where we met Chris Dickey, a correspondent for the Washington Post, who at the time was covering the Sandinistas' activities in Nicaragua. His home was in Washington DC, and he had an apartment in Mexico City. He was a fascinating man.

He said he used San Jose as his safe haven. Chris, as of late, is the Paris Bureau Chief for *Newsweek* magazine. Additionally, he is *Newsweek*'s Middle East Regional Editor. He's an incredible journalist. He has always jumped at the chance to be on the front line of news, no matter how dangerous. Just like he's doing right now in the middle of the most violent times the Middle East has ever seen. Chris' famous father, James Dickey, wrote the unforgettable book *Deliverance,* and the screenplay for the blockbuster movie, starring Bert Reynolds and John Voigt, that followed.

Michael and I thoroughly enjoyed the rapport we developed with Chris. From time to time, other journalists from a variety of high-caliber publications would drop in for a cold one and to discuss the Central American political scene with Chris. A couple of times, Michael and I got to share in the conversations. It was exciting.

We were in the company of great reporters with fearless ambition. It was fun to be his running partners, as we were, for a minute of our lives.

Just before we parted company, with Chris heading south to Managua, he gave me a country song he had written that he had jotted down on a yellow-lined tablet called "I'm Drunk and Disorderly Again."

He said if I ever got a chance to pass it on to a country singer to make a record out of it, he'd appreciate it. I've reproduced it below:

Drunk and Disorderly, Again
By Chris Dickey

I'm drunk and disorderly again,

Drinking with strangers and fightin' with my friends.

But no matter what I do,

I'm caught by thoughts of you.

I can't forget the lovin' we've been through.

I sit up all night drinking

With folks I've never seen.

Liquor makes some social,

But it just makes me mean.

If I chance to meet a friend of mine

Who wants to take me home,

I'll cuss him or swing at him

'til he leaves me alone.

'Cause I'm drunk and disorderly again…

Drinking with strangers and fightin' with my friends.

I've been to jail a few times.

Been warned off many more.

I've woke up in the gutter

And on the barroom floor.

I've spent countless mornings

Picking glass out of my hair,

Searching for a memory

And hoping it's not there.

I was drunk and disorderly again.

Drinking with strangers and fightin' with my friends.

You used to wait up, crying

For me to stagger home.

Then you said you'd leave me
Drunken and alone.
Late one Friday evening,
The lights at home weren't on,
And even before I opened the door,
I knew that you had gone.

I was drunk and disorderly again.
My drinking ways had lost me my best friend
Now no matter what I do,
How much whiskey I go through,
I know I'll never find another you.

I guess what stood out more than anything in the song is that it described some glaring aspects of my life. I had never been able to have meaningful relationships because I knew my drinking would eventually screw them up.

I woke up one morning at the Irazu Hotel with the bellboy beating on my door. He said I had a call from the USA. I hobbled down the hall to the front desk, and the guy motioned me to a phone on a table in a small nook of the front lobby.

It was a call from Kelly McCann, the program director of KSET in El Paso, Texas. Kelly had heard I was in San Jose and said he needed me for the next rating book. I didn't know much about Kelly, except that he knew his way around a radio station and was a good program director.

So, here I was in Costa Rica. The English-speaking station never did pan out. McCann says he needs me ASAP, and besides, I was tired of screwing around in San Jose anyway. Chris was leaving and Michael was headed back to Utah.

On the phone, McCann asked, "Can you be here in two days?"

I laughed and said, "Hey, man, I'm in the jungles of Central America. They only have two flights a week outta here."

He laughed and said, "Call me when you get back into town, and I'll tell you which motel we have set up."

I told him it would be about a week.

Chapter 39
One More Paso

Summers in El Paso are great. It's hot during the day, but a nice cool breeze blows in the evenings, and there are a million stars in the sky. KSET put me up at the Executive Inn, down the street from the station.

The May family, who had had some extraordinary success in Las Vegas in advertising, owned KSET. They bought some radio stations in Las Vegas, Albuquerque, and El Paso. Jerry May was the boss, father, and an all-around great guy. He had his kids, a son and two daughters, and his son-in-law involved, and everyone got along really well.

I was the afternoon guy. They paid me really well, and all of us on the air were having the time of our lives. Once again, my apartment had a huge bay window overlooking the entire city of El Paso and Juarez. It was ideal.

A week before the ratings began in mid-September, Monty Lang called from Majic 102 in Houston, the sister station to Majic 108 that I had worked for in St. Louis just a few months before.

"Monty Lang here," he said over the phone. "I need you. Why don't you come over and do mornings for me in Houston."

I was actually surprised that he wanted me to work for him after bolting from St. Louis like I did.

I couldn't make any serious money in El Paso and I hadn't given up the dream of being somebody. I wanted to be the top radio guy in a major city, so I simply said, "Eighty-five thousand."

"Eighty thousand, and I'll trade you out an apartment," he replied.

"Done!"

"Can you be here by Friday?"

Chapter 40
Look Who's Number One

I really felt like a jerk for leaving Jerry May in the lurch with only a few days before the fall rating book. I had to though. I had really wasted a couple of valuable career years playing around in El Paso. It was time to get back on the pony ride to fame and fortune.

Later, I found out that Jerry May had called Monty Lang and expressed his anger that they would hire me away from them so close to a rating book. I especially felt bad for letting Jerry down, period. Jerry was a heck of a guy.

I had been to Houston before, but I didn't notice how steamy it was. Sam Houston was a cousin, and my Texas mother had told me the history behind the city, but I couldn't figure out why anyone in his right mind, many years ago, would stand in the middle of that steamy swamp with cockroaches as big as your fist, and mosquitoes as large as birds, and say, "Let's build a city here."

God it was hot, and when it rained, it only took about thirty minutes to flood the entire city. Ah, but it was exciting. The city was on the move and it was hip, modern, and sophisticated. The women were outstandingly sexy—gorgeous, with a bit of a Texas accent. It was perfect.

Out on Richmond Avenue in Houston, just west of downtown, there was an English pub. The morning guys from KILT FM would hang out there. They called themselves Hudson and Harrigan. It was out of the ordinary, because no matter whom they hired, the show was still called "Hudson & Harrigan."

Fred Kennedy was Harrigan this time around. He was an extraordinary talent, a master at impressions, and extraordinary at writing comedy, which is a must if you're doing a fun-based morning show.

After I got off work at ten AM, I'd show up for breakfast, which was a pint of beer and Scottish eggs. Occasionally, I'd run into Fred there and thoroughly enjoy his company.

I liked drinking beer and joking with Fred. As big a talent as he was, he was humble and generous with comments. As usual, on a typical day, I drank my way into the afternoon, said goodbye to Fred, and welcomed the early evening crowd to the pub, usually half in the bag at that point and bitching about the bad breaks I had to endure.

The Majic 102 studios were on Richmond Avenue also, but closer to Houston, just west of downtown. Jim Maddox had built a great radio station, but they couldn't find a morning man who could make it work for them. It was my turn. The sound of Jim's music formula was fabulous. This time he had streamlined it for me, so I didn't need a slide rule and calculator to figure it out. No one in town could hope to sound as hip as we did. We had a great combination of the hippest of the urban favorites, with a little soft jazz. Man, it sizzled. I poured it on. I won the ratings battle that fall, beating everyone in town.

The major competition was the country station, called KICK FM. Their morning team had been on top for years, but not this time. It was *my* time. I was about to be somebody.

I was lucky enough to score some of the highest ratings in recent Houston radio history. I loved it, but within a year, they felt they could do without Jim Maddox, the founder of the Majic format.

They put our midday guy in charge, a DJ who had never run anything before, and who once sold peanuts at the Astrodome. "Peanuts. Get your peanuts right here." His name was Bill. When he was appointed Program Director, we all felt happy for him. He had always been really nice and polite, and he had a great voice. Ah ha!

Things were about to change. Bill must have been waiting his whole life to boss somebody around, and this was his chance. "Introducing Mr. My Way or the Highway." We all began calling him "Master Sergeant Bill."

This guy was a complete jackass, and was about to run many of us off. He changed from a guy who would come in early to spend friendly time with everyone to a full-fledged prick.

Bill was determined to tame me, even if he had to ruin the morning show in the process. One morning, he called me on the hotline to tell me that he didn't like something I had said on the air. I told him not to screw with me while I was doing the show and went back to work. He called back and told me that when I got off he wanted to see me, and that I was in a lot of trouble.

Whatever it was that Master Sergeant Bill didn't like when he heard it apparently had Monty Lang, our GM, in stitches, because the moment Bill came in and brought it up to Lang, Monte started laughing and said, "Wasn't that the most hilarious thing you every heard?"

I think Bill must have told him, "Yeah," because he came into the control room and said, "Never mind the meeting when you get

off. That was a funny bit after all, but don't tell me to 'stick it' again."
Monty told me of their exchange later that morning. Bill was such an
ass wipe; I could see the road was getting rocky. They couldn't have
higher ratings in the morning. What the hell does he want?

Chapter 41
Mary, Queen of Scotch

Our sales manager at Majic 102 was a walk on the wild side. Her name was Mary Ann. She was pretty, and brilliant in the world of radio ad sales. I did her a few favors for clients, like producing a special radio ad for them, and she appreciated it.

I couldn't help but notice that she kept stealing glances of me, so it came as no surprise when she asked if I wanted to join her for happy hour later one afternoon. I was up for it, but I wanted to avoid another calamity like the one that had happened in St. Louis. I'd have to date one at a time here.

Our first date was interesting. She owned a little condo inside the loop in Houston—a term used to describe the close-in location, as it gave you privileges. All it really meant was that you didn't have to navigate the horrendous traffic on the loop every rush hour.

Mary Ann invited me in with a kiss on the cheek, looking very nice and smelling great. The beer she offered was a long-neck Lone Star, a

Texas favorite. Mary Ann asked if I wanted something a little stronger. I asked her what she meant. She said, "Pull open the drawer just next to and under the sink." When I did, I saw an incredible variety of recreational items. Several pre-rolled joints, a vial of cocaine, some powder in a little envelope that later I found out was ecstasy, and a large plug of hash waiting to be smoked.

Mary Ann was the daughter of a prominent El Paso businessman, so we both had roots in the same place. Her father got rich supplying public restrooms across the state with hand towels, soap, urinal cakes, and the like. They had a beautiful, luxurious home off Scenic Drive in El Paso, where the well to do all had their homes.

Mary Ann and I were married shortly thereafter, which was the beginning of an unbelievably rocky marriage. I would find out that Mary Ann had a wide variety of suitors who came a knockin' early in the morning after the bars closed. She'd chase them away, and act like she was embarrassed.

After a few drinks, she flirted with everyone. She didn't stop, even on our honeymoon in Puerto Vallarta, Mexico. I couldn't believe it; she was shameless. On the night before we left for Mexico, she hit on my brother. He reluctantly told me so later.

If I said anything like, "Maybe you should slow down a bit," she would become violent. I called it her "party threshold." Man, that pissed her off. I always said, "If any woman I'm married to cheats on me, that's it. I'm gone."

I now found myself in the same position that many of the women in my life had found themselves. I also bought into her lies of denying her infidelity.

One Saturday afternoon at our condo inside the loop, she'd been drinking and taking God knows what. She was sitting on our couch, drink in hand, talking about wanting to go visit with her girlfriend, which meant that she was thinking about one of her usual suitors and was about to go get laid.

I was standing in front of her when I said, "Please don't go out screwing around on me. You're in your party mode again."

Before I could react, she kicked me hard in the ribs, cracking three of them. I should have called the cops on her right then and there, because that became a habit. She got me good.

I was miserable and could hardly move without pain for several weeks. Many times, when I wasn't looking, she'd haul off and sucker punch me in the face.

The parade of men, the violence, and later, the meanness of our relationship lasted almost five agonizing years. It was another wake up call for me, as I was chalking this marriage up to karma.

I tolerated her abuse because, as usual, I needed an enabler. I wanted someone who would hold me accountable for my drinking, but who would allow me to disappear into my alcoholic nightmare from time to time without throwing me out of the house.

I needed someone to forgive me when I screwed up. So, it stands to reason, then, that I was her enabler as well. I can't tell you how many times we separated and got back together. She would usually instigate another horrendous fight, I'd leave, and after a few days or weeks, she'd come begging for my forgiveness.

I would forgive her, and then she'd forgive me. Back and forth it went, year after year. She was wealthy and, selfishly, it was easy to get comfortable as a kept man. Sanity was out of the question.

In addition to my morning show, I began writing comedy for other morning shows across the country and started a company to sell it called "DJ Comedy Service."

It was a little different than the other services available, which focused primarily on morning shows, in that I wrote lines usable by

DJs in other day parts, such as lines relative to song titles, intros, and outros. The service did all right, but it was time consuming.

I spent most of my waking hours each day trying to think of cutting-edge comedy. Being funny is serious business. Writing comedy was good though, because when Master Sgt. Travis had finally gotten on my last nerve and I couldn't stand it anymore, John Lander, a client of mine from Miami, told me he was coming to Houston and wanted to know if I'd be his partner.

Lander was an extraordinary talent. He was very handsome, and he had a gift of gab and a natural curiosity that made him a very interesting and popular guy. He came with a great reputation, so I felt like maybe, at last, the Gods were blessing me.

Chapter 42
Oh, God! Tell Me I Didn't Say That!

In the interim, before Lander came to Houston, I was offered a job at KRBE, a Top 40 station in Houston. Barry Kaye was our afternoon talent. He had been named *Billboard* magazine's major market "Radio Personality of the Year" a few years back. He was a fabulous DJ, but even more, he was a singer, a la Tom Jones.

He appeared three or four nights a week at the Ramada Inn in Houston. It was a very progressive venue. By that time, I had gotten my old friend, John Rio (Carrillo), hired at KRBE. One night Rio and I decided we'd go catch Barry's show. Needless to say, when we arrived, we were already stoned and in the bag.

Barry invited us into his room for a blast of something. All my old friends were there: Johnny, Jack, and Jose. I'm not sure, but I think we had a shot of each before Barry asked me to do a stand-up routine in between shows.

I told him, "Sure." I was a little nervous about it because I wasn't fully prepared, but I sat through Barry's set, working on my comedy road map. I was ready when he introduced me, and from there, my memory is sketchy. Apparently, I pulled it off. I called John Rio down on to the stage and had him do an improvised routine with me as well. I introduced Rio as Juan de La Garza, one of the foremost Flamenco guitarists in the world, who just happened to be in our audience.

I pressed the audience to clap for a short performance by The Maestro. Rio, finally, came down on stage, apologized in a well-rehearsed Spanish accent for the casualness of his dress, as he wasn't expecting to be performing.

He sat down in a chair, center stage, with an acoustic guitar that one of the guys in the band had loaned him. He played an extraordinary Flamenco riff and then backed down for a minute, and with an anguished look on his face, dramatically said, "Aye!" He mumbled some words in Spanish that all ran together, but sounded like he was expressing his anguish.

He played another riff, followed by another really loud "Aye!" that was again followed by a string of meaningless Spanish words in rapid succession that seemed to be a reflection of his extraordinary mental pain.

At last, he looked up at the crowd, played a very melodic series of Flamenco notes, paused as if he were going to cry, and then yelled, "Aye … Choo!" He sneezed.

The crowd went berserk with laughter. It was Rio's first on-stage comedy bit, and he pulled it off in a big way. Funny, that's one of the only elements of the evening I remember.

Barry said we were hilarious, but all I remembered was Rio's bit and some guy in the audience slapping me on the back as I walked off stage. Good Lord! I did a comedy set on stage, in a full blackout and pulled it off. This was very dangerous, as it would encourage me to not worry how much I drank, because the outcome would work itself out.

About a week later, Barry was the emcee at The Hotspot Club in Houston and asked me along. Barry was a very congenial host who had the people at the nightclub eating out of his hand. He introduced me to the crowd and I got a great round of applause. The remote was over at 10:00 PM, and then Barry and a few others decided to have a Tequila Slammin' contest. As usual, I was already half in the bag, so when I got to the third Cuervo, I was done for. I morphed into a complete blackout. Barry left, and I was very close to passing out.

This wouldn't be good. I was so drunk that I couldn't stand on my own. I slightly remember hearing someone say, "That's Brad Edwards from KRBE." People were pointing and shaking their heads. A trio of partners owned the club, one of whom was Asian. As they were trying to stuff me into a cab, I went on a drunken diatribe saying, "What a shame we didn't get the rest of you Viet Cong sons of bitches in Nam while we had the chance."

Oh, God. The club was a big client of KRBE's. I was so drunk and stoned that I couldn't tell the cab driver where I lived, who I was, or anything else. Somehow, after a lengthy time and a ton of patience on everyone's part, I was finally able to pull enough clarity from deep within my alcohol-soaked brain to remember my phone number. Mary Ann showed up, embarrassed and angry, because she had done business with the club herself.

Needless to say, the club owners weren't amused and wanted my ass fired. The next day was a Saturday and I was sick and devastated by my behavior the night before. That evening, I called the club and was able to talk to Joe, the Asian owner I had so insulted. I apologized unconditionally, which he accepted, but very coldly. What else could I expect? Monday morning I was fired. So much for being somebody.

I had only been with KRBE for three months when John Lander came to town. He and I hit it off well. I failed to mention the KRBE incident at the club. As a matter of fact, I don't think I even mentioned that I had worked for KRBE. What an embarrassing turn in my life.

Chapter 43
The "Q Morning Zoo"

Lander; Patty Hamilton, who was our music director and also Lander's significant other; and myself met and planned our attack. The biggest challenge would be to take the market over with KULF 790. It's nearly impossible to win a market with an AM station doing music, but Lander assured me that we were going to be doing something really different. He was very charismatic and I bought into it.

Our sister station in Tampa, Florida had launched a new format with Scott Shannon and the "Q Morning Zoo" that had taken the market by storm. If we were to succeed with the new 79 Q, we'd get 93.1 FM. That was the company promise.

Shannon had developed the "Zoo" format with Cleveland Wheeler, his partner, in Tampa, Florida, and it was the most innovative new idea in radio to come along since Bill Drake gave us Boss Radio. We would be the second Zoo in the United States. Lander felt we could get good ratings right away. If we did, we'd get the FM station as promised.

I'll never forget the first morning on the air in August of '82. Scott Shannon flew up for the launch of the 79 Q Zoo in the morning. Charlie Van Dyke, a well-known personality and our group program director, who had one of the deepest and most beautiful voices in the world, was also there from our flagship station in Virginia.

We also had "Flash," our traffic guy, and "Clete Dumpster" doing sports. Each of us, with our special talents, came together for an absolute hit and then some. That first morning on the air was controlled mayhem.

Shannon was so creative. So Lander and I basically played along as Shannon taught us the ropes of the Q Morning Zoo. Listeners in Houston were just blown away with the originality of the show. We knew immediately that we had a hit.

We set the town on fire and went to first place in the ratings in ninety days, with an AM radio station. That was unheard of at that point. We were the talk of the town.

All of us were bona-fide stars and the company kept their promise. We began working on the FM, turning the AM over to our other local talent, like Barry Kaye, our "Bud," who was chosen as the top DJ in the country and who sang like Tom Jones.

We would simulcast the Q Zoo In The Morning on both stations—79 Q AM and 93 Q FM.

The more I continued to write comedy, one-liners mainly, the more I wanted to see how it would go over in front of a live audience, so I began showing up at the Comix Annex in Houston doing a stand-up act.

Stand-up can be brutal, especially since I was the new guy and had to go on last for a while. By the time I got on, I had better be funny. The audience was drunk and they were looking to heckle you off the stage. Surprisingly, I only bombed a few times.

One night, Sam Keniston showed up. He was a God at The Annex. He was incredible. No one heckled Sam or he'd have your ass. His comedy was deep, original, and almost embarrassingly personal, but very funny!

I had a chance to talk with Sam back stage for a minute, and he told me to, "Take them on. Don't let them take you on." He added, "Be ready for anything. Some nights you can hit them with your best shit and they love it, and the next time you come back, with the same stuff, they stick it up your ass."

He was right; comedy is tough. The comedy I wrote that worked at the Comix Annex went on the air with the Q Zoo In the Morning.

Working with Lander was interesting. He had a great personality and was naturally curious, which is good because he was always inquisitive when we were interviewing someone or talking with listeners on the phone.

The studios were in the penthouse of a skyscraper in downtown Houston. We looked down over Highway 59, the main freeway, knifing its way through town. We had an incredible view.

Just before we went on the air each morning, like clockwork, one of us would pull out a joint and nod his head at the door leading out to the roof. Out we'd go. Some of us hit the door, willing to let the chips fall where they would after getting stoned. It was crazy. We went on the air ripped out of our minds, with Lander, who didn't partake, spending the morning directing us through the clouds. It was insane.

It had been almost a year and 79Q and 93Q were cooking. Once again, faced with success, I began drinking quite a bit. I don't know if I was trying to sabotage myself, or if I just liked getting drunk. The bottom line was, I was having a difficult time getting to work so early in the morning. One morning, I was so passed out that I didn't call in as I slept through the alarm. Lander called and asked what had happened and I was honest with him. He said, "Don't do it again. I don't want to have to let you go." Wow, that hit me like a ton of bricks.

Then, it happened. A week later, I didn't wake up for the alarm again. Lander let me go. I was destroyed. Our show had just been highlighted in *Newsweek* magazine a few weeks earlier, and now, I'm gone. I could see it coming, like a train wreck you can't stop, no matter how much you wave and scream.

What a loser. Mary Ann and I were in the middle of another break up, and I didn't have my enabler to help me wake up in the morning. I was blown away.

Chapter 44
Please, Help Me

I was lost for days, wondering what to do with myself. I was pretty much screwed in Houston. My reputation had fully caught up with me. Just when I thought my career was all but over, Jhani Kaye offered me some work at KFI radio station in Los Angeles.

I flew back and forth to L.A. for a few weeks, ending up working for Jhani for most of the summer of 1983. "Too Shy" by Kajagoogoo, "Total Eclipse of the Heart" by Bonnie Tyler, and "True" by Spandau Ballet were some of the first hits I played on KFI.

It was good to be back home in Los Angeles. Jhani, my old friend, was very loyal. He gave me enough work to keep me busy. I even got the privilege of filling in for the famous Loman and Barkley. I decided to work on myself, and get sober once and for all. Mary Ann said that she had found someone who would buy our condo in Houston. So be it.

In what amounted to one of life's little oddities, my ex-wife Arlene asked me if I'd house-sit for her in Santa Monica for the summer, as she and her husband-to-be, Tom, would be heading for a long road vacation through Canada. I jumped at the chance, and that began my long road to recovery.

Alcoholics and their families hear, "We have to reach our bottom before recovery can begin." A person has to be wrung out, beaten down, and hurting so bad that he becomes so "sick and tired of being sick and tired" that he finally faces the honesty of the situation. The key word is *honesty*.

There is one line in my program that continued to roll around in my pea brain, aggravating me like a pebble in my shoe. I paraphrase: There are some people who will never recover, because they won't give their all to the program, usually individuals who lack the capacity to be completely honest with themselves.

We have to ruin countless marriages, relationships, and friendships before we can begin to see the bottom. Moreover, we have to take ourselves down so low that we are helpless and hopeless.

Many of us sink to levels that we had previously not thought possible. If I ever get *that* bad, I'll quit drinking. I was at that point, close to flat broke, and mentally and physically bankrupt.

Like I mentioned earlier from my alcoholic program: Most alcoholics believe that one day they'll be able to get a grip on their drinking. It's an incredible obsession. Many alcoholics chase this belief to their to destruction and even death.

I was finally ready to take the first step. It was difficult admitting I had no power over alcohol and that I couldn't manage my life and affairs. What a revelation. Oh, how many times I thought about that and always held a little reservation that, "Maybe I'm really not that bad." Now I'm thinking, "If I can face the facts of my life honestly, then, and only then, will I be able to change them."

I headed for Los Angeles to work at KFI and attend meetings for alcoholics every chance I got, not to mention that I replanted Arlene's lawn and landscaped her yard that summer. It was therapeutic. It was like a continuous opportunity to think.

I wanted sobriety so badly, but I wasn't able to "let go absolutely." I began heading down another dangerous road. I could intellectualize my alcoholism, but I could only stay sober for short lengths of time, maybe sixty to ninety days, and then out I went for a couple of more shots of misery.

Usually, it would be one afternoon of drinking, and then I would come right back to the meetings, admitting my failure. I didn't have anywhere else to go. I had lost all my friends, and two marriages. By this time, anyone who loved me was long gone.

I felt so lonely. There were always the superficial relationships, better known as one-night stands, but those just seemed to make me lonelier.

The hole got deeper within me. I gave serious thought to suicide at that point. "If I can't get sober, I don't want to live like this anymore," I thought. I felt that The Lord had something else in mind for me. It was that personal revelation that kept me from doing myself in.

Soon enough, I was offered a very good job back in El Paso. Whenever I was filling in at night on KFI, which has one of the most powerful signals in the USA, some of the radio guys would listen to me in El Paso. From my previous radio successes, I had a large fan base, as they had pretty much had adopted me as one of their own in that fine West-Texas town.

The offer was for mornings, and I knew that if I was going to succeed, it would be as a morning man, not as a relief man at KFI. Prestigious as it was, I told Jhani "No." He was surprised, but he understood. I love Jhani. He'll never know how he saved my life.

One of the reason's Ron Haney, the program director at B94 FM in El Paso, wanted me to work for him because his midday personality, Dave Jeffries, was drinking a lot. Ron knew that I was having some success staying sober, so he thought that I might be able to help Dave come around. What a dangerous situation.

I was barely sober and Haney wanted me to help Dave Jeffries. Haney had been our chief engineer at the Q Zoo in Houston, and had gotten the job as program director at B94 FM. He was a likable guy who knew why I had been fired by Lander and supported my effort to get sober.

Mary Ann called when she heard I was back in El Paso and said she felt that we hadn't given our marriage a real opportunity to succeed, that she had been working on herself, and that, coupled with my desire to really quit drinking, we should get back together. Mistake number four thousand, and I went for it.

B94 FM was situated in an office above a bank, close to the University of Texas at El Paso. I worked on my morning show day and night. I wanted to get good, popular, and quick, so I could get back to the majors as quickly as possible. I was popular in El Paso, but I had to make B94 FM my last stand, because listeners were growing weary of my moving around so much. When I wasn't working, I was going to alcoholics meetings.

I began to feel better about life in general. I wish I could say the same for Dave Jeffries. As I signed off at ten AM, he would acknowledge me through bloodshot eyes and then sit down for a five-hour drunk on the air.

He was getting so drunk on the air; it was difficult to decipher what he was saying. I called Haney during one such horrific diatribe and said, "Dave's drunk as a skunk. Shouldn't you take him off the air?"

Haney said that he was taping it and that he would play it back for Dave, hoping to shame him into sobriety.

I told Haney it wouldn't work. It was embarrassing listening to him trying to work his way in and out of the songs and commercials.

Dave had been a fabulous talent working for Bill Drake, the creator of Boss Radio, as one of their talents and program directors. Dave once was the program director at KYNO, Fresno, one of Drakes clipper stations.

He turned me down more than once when I tried to get hired there, but he was kind to me and I always liked him. It was very sad to see him deteriorate to this point, but the manager of B94 FM, Craig Parker, decided to give him one last chance, sending him to a twenty-eight-day alcoholic rehab program.

Jeffries came back, looking about twenty pounds heavier, which was good, since he had been down to skin and bones. His eyes were clear, and he had a hopeful look on his face. I couldn't have been happier for him.

Then, after about two weeks, he was drinking again. Sadly, B94 FM had to let him go. They had given him every chance possible. Jeffries threw everything he owned into the back of his AMC Pacer and headed for his dad's home in Utah.

A few nights later, he stuck the barrel of a shotgun into his mouth and blew his head off. He was a great guy who, like me, couldn't stop drinking.

Chapter 45
Footsteps in the Sand

One of the must do's in my program for alcoholics was working on the spiritual side of your life, finding a Higher Power. I had always believed in God, but felt that he had turned his back on me when he "allowed" me to become an alcoholic.

I don't doubt that I was born an alcoholic; it had been in the family for several generations. Certainly, I was predestined to be one all my life. So, step one of my alcoholics program, admitting I was an alcoholic, was a given, even though I kept modifying it to fit my style of a so-called program.

I admitted that I was an alcoholic and that my life was unmanageable, but the next step is about finding a power greater than us, and discovering how that power can restore our sanity.

All right, if the Lord had allowed me to be born this way, then why do I have to believe that he would restore me to sanity? I believed that

I was never sane in the first place, so how would I ever recognize sanity when it arrived.

I was born with a bucket full of "isms" that wrecked and ruined my entire life, up that point. So that controlled my attitude for a long time. Of course, it's just another hurdle I erected to keep myself from finding sobriety, completely. How can you be returned to something you've never known?

No. In my mind, I had been cheated. My concept of a Higher Power was then, as it is now, God, his Son, Jesus Christ, and the Holy Spirit. My father said that he was an atheist, pointing to *his* father's behavior and thinking. How could a Baptist minister working for the Lord do the things he did?

Dad spent his life trying to disprove the Lord's existence; ultimately, though, I think he died a believer. Mom, on the other hand, was a wonderful Christian woman. She sent us kids to church, and, every summer, to Bible school down at the local Assembly of God.

Our next-door neighbors in Grants Pass, Oregon, the Stanger's, were Mormon—all nine of them. I even attended their services from time to time. I admired the warm, genuine friendliness and great family values that Mormons lived. All that Mom wanted was for us to know God and Jesus and their goodness.

I recommitted to the Lord when I was very young, but I turned my back on God, deciding I would do life on my terms.

Dave Jeffries unnecessary death scared me. The Lord wanted me to see this example, I was sure. At that moment, though, on one particular night at alcoholic men's only meeting, I was wondering how to get back in touch with God. My way wasn't working, and if I had to make a deal with the Lord, I was ready. I was afraid that I wouldn't be able to grasp the simple program as it was being shown to me.

So, someone brought up the existence of God for the billionth time at that AA meeting. I complained how it seemed that there was no higher power in my life working to save me, when an old man, a member who had been sober for many years, stood up in the middle of my confused rant and said, "I'll tell you how I got back on track, and it was easy. When you go home tonight, get down on your knees and simply ask him for help, and then wait for the answer," he continued. "It may not come tonight, or tomorrow, but it will come," he concluded.

It's important to note that I didn't want to do it. I just did it anyway, hoping against hope that it might work. I always had a problem with religious dogma—things like, "Get down on your knees and witness to the Lord Jesus Christ," usually expressed by some weird-looking idiot with a southern accent. To me, those words came from the mouths of fanatics.

I thought about what the old-timer had said. What could it hurt? "Just ask." I had not asked for God's help, other than the usual, "God, if you'll get me out of this one, I'll never do it again," in years. "Just ask." And ask I did that night by my bedside in El Paso, Texas.

I remember feeling somewhat embarrassed down on my knees, kind of nervous that Mary Ann might come home and see me. I folded my hands and asked God to forgive me for turning my back on him. I couldn't stop crying.

I poured thirty years of tears into my conversation with the Lord that night, and I'm telling you, slowly, my life began to change. I knew that it was the Lord working on me, but often, I'd chalk it up to coincidence. It's amazing how many coincidences came my way after asking the Lord to help me. To paraphrase "Footsteps in the Sand," when I thought he had forsaken me and there was only one set of footsteps in the sand, I wasn't walking alone; he was carrying me.

Needless to say, this spoke directly to my heart. I found a sponsor and started working on sobriety. Sponsors are men and women who have a lot of sobriety and who work a daily program of recovery themselves. These individuals, who work a strong program, can help get you on the right road so that your recovery will be done the right way.

Living by these simple steps is not easy. Sponsors are there to help you understand the alcoholic program, interpret the steps and what you might need to know to work them properly, and stay sober. Sponsors are there to help you when you need them. Men help men, and women help women.

Early on in the program, a newcomer doesn't really know what to do next. We came in confused, beaten down, and sucking on our last straw. Selecting a sponsor is as simple as hearing someone at a meeting whom you respect or identify with. I always suggest to a newcomer, first ask if a person will be your temporary sponsor. That way, if it doesn't work out, it was just temporary and you can continue to look for someone with whom you're compatible.

A sponsor is the one person you tell everything to. Ernie was my first sponsor, and I couldn't have had a better one. He knew every scam and sham, every excuse, every everything that I could ever try to pull on him.

When I felt I'd been wronged about something, he'd mock me by saying, "Aw, poor me, poor me, pour me a drink."

"There's no such thing as justified anger," he'd say. "If you want to keep drinking, then go out and get even, or shut the fuck up about it." He would slam my escape routes closed immediately. Then, we'd discuss it. I trusted him completely.

Ernie's direction is instilled deeply within me. When something comes up about behavior, I can hear Ernie saying,

"Work that tenth step of AA man before you go out and get drunk." He was referring to when we screw up, we should admit it, say we're sorry, and continue. It's about getting rid of anger and knowing when you're wrong so resentments won't build up.

I trusted Ernie with my life. He was the only guy who could talk to me like that and have me feeling grateful for the gift of his admonishment—peckerhead. Ernie was an ex-Marine, if there is such a thing. He'd been through hell in Korea and I respected him. He could be tough, as most Leather Necks can be, but that's exactly what I needed.

I was going to a lot of meetings before I chose a sponsor. I was attending three, sometimes four meetings a day. What impressed me was that Ernie was at most of those meetings too, and he had been sober for twelve years at the time.

When I first approached him, he said that he was working with too many guys as it was, but I poured it on. I told him that I needed him, and that he was one of the only guys in the program I could relate to. What got him was when I said, "If you don't take me in, I'll have a drunk for a sponsor. *Me.*"

It wasn't a new line; it was just the right time to say it. He said, "Okay, but don't screw up."

I love him. He's still in El Paso, keeping drunks off the streets. I'd like to tell you his story, but it's all I can do to remember mine.

Sobriety was finally beginning to work for me. I still had the compulsion to drink, but I persevered on hope. Hope that one day I too could be compulsion free and that my program strength would make me strong enough to carry me over the period in between. What a dream. I knew that I was still in trouble, but I was going to meetings and not drinking in between and I was putting off until tomorrow the need for the next drink, which was all I could hope for at the time.

I heard a lady in an AA meeting say, "If you think willpower has anything to do with not drinking, the next time you have diarrhea, try to hold it in. It's the same thing." I thought it was a beautiful line. So many of us are told, "You have to have strong willpower to quit drinking." No, it's a disease.

I was a huge success on B94 FM, but there was a problem. I was sober, but I was having trouble with something I'd heard about one of our bosses. One of the other DJs told me that he came back to the station late one night and caught him fondling a young boy.

That blew me away. "A dirty, rotten, child molesting predator—unforgivable!" I was so filled with my own rage that it didn't occur to me that it could be a lie. I didn't run in and accuse anyone as I had no real proof, but the stories from the DJ were rocking my world.

I was very naïve in my early days of sobriety. I was being as honest about everything as I could, and I mistakenly thought that everyone else was too. My source was also telling me stories about how he knew that our GM was screwing off and wasn't really working at all. I bought it all. So, I quit. It was a big mistake, proving that, even sober, I could make mistakes.

I really poured on the meetings. There was a 10:00 AM meeting in El Paso, as well as one at noon, 5:00 PM, 8:00 PM, and even a 10:00 PM meeting on Saturday nights. My sponsor, Ernie, and I were playing racquetball two or three times a week. My mental, spiritual, and physical health were improving rapidly, and I felt good.

I had finally gotten six straight months of continuous sobriety, which was a huge milestone. Mary Ann began selling real estate and doing well, so as a gift for reaching six months of sobriety, she bought me an old 1951 Buick I'd been eyeballing, which I began rebuilding. Life was finally looking up.

I began doing fill-in work on KSET. The Mays were selling it, and it was just floating in the market place without any rudder. The GM didn't care; he was just holding down the fort until it sold. It didn't matter though, because I was working to develop air checks to send out, in hopes of getting back into the majors.

One afternoon, I was back in the copy room at KSET where Shirley Skinner was doing some work. She was our business manager at the station. Shirley was Amerasian. Her father had taken a "Japanese war bride." Shirley had a nice figure, but it was her face that attracted me. I told her in the copy room that afternoon that she had one of the prettiest faces I'd ever seen. She blushed and thanked me, which led to a lunch together in a few days.

She became smitten with me, and I was fascinated by her too, but the timing was all off. I was still married to the infamous Mary Ann and Shirley was married to a professor at New Mexico State University, about fifty miles away in Las Cruces.

At last, thanks to my program for alcoholism I was beginning to believe that I could count on myself. As usual, Mary Ann and I were at odds with one another. This time because she was still drinking and doing a variety of drugs, and there were the usual unexplained absences. It was all behavior that I really wanted nothing to do with anymore.

Chapter 46
Miami Nice

In September of 1985, at seven months sober, I was offered the job as morning man and team leader for the Q Morning Zoo in Miami, Florida, at a radio station called I95.

It was named after the main highway that runs from Maine to the tip of Florida. I95 had long been the only hit station in Miami, and they decided to take the morning show in a different direction.

When I flew down to Miami to meet Keith Isley, the program director, there was electricity in the air. "Miami Vice" was the top TV show and the "Miami Vice" theme was number one on the music charts. It was exhilarating.

Miami was a very hip and beautiful place. We put together a good deal for a couple of years, and I signed the contract and then headed home to El Paso to get my gear. Mary Ann was happy, but wouldn't be able to come down for a while. It was just as well. I had work to do.

Bill Taylor would be my sidekick. Bill was a comedy writer, impressionist, radio personality, and an old friend of mine, whom I had known since my Los Angeles and Houston days. As we did in Houston, I set up the show with a traffic person, Lisa Lisa, who did entertainment and commentary, and news with Herb Sierra.

The show kicked into gear fairly well, but Taylor was a little out of touch. His sense of humor was not cutting edge. He delivered corny lines and talked incessantly. I had to put my foot down on the Bing Crosby impressions. "That was years ago, Bill," I told him. "It's a great impression, but now is now, and that was then."

It was kind of like having your dad on the show with you. I was having a difficult time keeping him on mark. If I didn't give him enough time on the microphone, he would literally howl like a dog. It was the craziest thing I'd ever seen.

I had to have the rest of the crew leave the control room a couple of times in order to get him straightened out. I was concerned. Keith Isley, our program director, who had been there for seven or eight years, up and quit in a dispute with the GM over something unrelated to the show.

Then, a week later, the GM quit. Oh, God. What did I do to deserve this? Most of the station's budget was going to Taylor, myself, and the rest of the show, so I knew that we'd be looked at long and hard.

On a personal level, Mary Ann came into town and immediately began hammering me over one thing or another. I told her, "Don't even unpack. Move on. Go straight to wherever you want to live, but not here." I had finally had it with her.

Communication with our morning team came down to a trickle, as we were without a captain. Then, sure enough, they brought in some old guy who had retired from the company some years before, just to watch over the operation, and hired some hayseed from the Quad Cities in Iowa to be the new program director.

His take on what worked for a morning show was so mid-western that his teeth looked like corn when he spoke. Few knew or understood the complexity of the Q Morning Zoo. That's why Scott Shannon and John Lander had been so successful, because they understood what it takes. I did too, but I was pretty sure that I wasn't going to get the power to prove it at I95.

Now, here I am, with a morning partner who's stuck in the '50s and '60s, I've just lost a PD who'd been there for years, who knew what to do and how, and we've got this jaggoff just in from the Corn Cities to tell us how it works. This guy's background was small-market Classic Rock, so the handwriting was on the wall. Taylor and I only stayed on until the end of January.

We were on the air the morning the Space Shuttle *Challenger* blew up. Dick Scobee, Michael Smith, Ronald McNair, Ellison Onizuka, Gregory Jarvis, and Judy Resnik, along with schoolteacher Christa McAuliffe, all died. Frank Motek from WINZ News, our sister station next door, came in and said, "Let me on. I have an urgent bulletin." I threw him the mic and he began the horrifying story of the plight of *Challenger*. We were all shocked speechless.

Space Shuttle *Challenger* disintegrated seventy-three seconds into its flight after an O-ring seal in its right solid rocket booster failed at liftoff. The seal failure caused a breach in the joint it filled, allowing a flare to reach the outside and impinge upon the adjacent attachment hardware and external fuel tank.

We could still see the plume of smoke in the sky, and we were almost 200 miles south of the Kennedy Space Center. It was an awful and sickening feeling for all of us. We spent hours writing tributes and having kids in from a local grade school to sing a tribute we wrote for the astronauts.

A week later, I95 took us off the air and negotiated a buy-out of our two-year contracts. We were more or less screwed, as we didn't have an extra dime to spend, so our negotiating wiggle room was non-existent.

When I moved to South Florida, I had rented a beautiful condo on one of the Miami Lakes, in a Miami suburb. Don Schula's golf course and restaurant were just down the street. It is a beautiful tropical paradise, and allowing Mary Ann to talk me into reconciliation had been another major mistake. Oh, but she wasn't through with me yet.

I95 cut me a check for $33,000. I stuck it in my briefcase and went to my condo on the lake. Mary Ann dropped by to tell me she was sorry it went so poorly and to wish me luck, or so I thought.

When I wasn't looking, she took the settlement check out of my briefcase because I stupidly mentioned it to her. She deposited it into our joint account, the one with only a few dollars in it, by writing, "For deposit only" on it and withdrew every dime. I didn't know it.

She then disappeared back to Texas, leaving me penniless. My God, what to do? I was devastated. Not knowing where to turn, I finally called my brother in San Jose, California and asked for a couple of thousand dollars to get by.

I quickly went job hunting again. Fortunately, I was hired right away to do fill in work at radio station WA1A, another radio station named after a Florida highway. A1A is the scenic highway that follows the coastline and the inter-coastal waterway—a beautiful drive. WA1A was adult contemporary. As it turned out, they were looking for a morning man, so we started the process of seeing if I was a fit.

Harry Lyles was the program director. He had been the PD for Steve Jost, the GM, when they were together in Columbus, Ohio.

Harry was a brother. He was very dapper and handsome, and he knew his stuff. I liked him, and he liked me, for a while.

The first thing Lyles did was take me in to get the okay from Jost so that he could put me on the air doing mornings temporarily. Then I had to get past the consultant. I was called in to meet with Harry, Jost, and the consultant. He looked me over, asked a few questions about where I'd been, what music I liked, and a bit about my lifestyle. We all shook hands, and I learned later from Harry that he had given his okay to hire me.

"One more step, Brad," Lyles went on. "Now, you have to meet the company shrink." I couldn't believe it, but it was true. We both laughed about it, but Cox wanted to look at the psychological profiles of the people they hired for important positions.

So, one day, Lyles had me come in to Steve Jost's office, where the company shrink asked me some questions. It was actually fun, but bizarre. That was Thursday, March 27, 1986. Afterward, I went home.

Lyles called again. He wanted me to, "Look good," and join him for one more meeting in Jost's office that Friday afternoon. When I walked in, Mr. Jost was there, with Lyles and the consultant. I sat down and Lyles stood up, smiled, and said,

"Gentlemen, meet our new morning man for WA1A."

Wow! Fabulous! They ordered some hors d'oeuvres, and when Lyles offered me a beer, I took it, drank it, and celebrated the beginning of the next downfall in my life on a day that should have been reserved for one of life's victories.

As I took a swallow of that beer and felt the coolness of the suds filling my mouth and throat that tasted so good, and the rush of the alcohol doing what made me feel happy, I told myself that this time, it'll be different. All the while rolling around in my sub-conscious was the thought, "Welcome to the end of any success you may have hoped for."

So there I was, just a couple weeks shy of my first year of sobriety, and my ducks were going in different directions. I was about to find myself in the middle of what many might think was a script for a made-for-TV Movie.

The following Monday morning when I came in to work, anticipating the signing of a multiyear contract, there was a memo in all our boxes introducing me as the new Morning personality on WA1A. There was another memo in there too, telling one and all that Steven Jost and his team had, "Decided to explore other opportunities."

Oh no, what about the contract we were supposed to sign that day? How 'bout Harry Lyles, Not another nightmare? I just went through this at I95.

Lyles came in that morning and told me that Cox had indeed let Jost go, and that we wouldn't have a contract because the company was reviewing what to do with the station. I felt like I was in "The Twilight Zone."

They kept us all on for a few more months. I would come in, do the morning show half-heartedly, and leave at ten AM, ready for a beer and lunch in Miami Lakes by eleven.

Just before summer, they let us all go and changed the name of the station to "The Gator," Which played Classic Rock. Here's $5,000, and now out the door you go. I couldn't believe it. How long will it be before I completely crack? Time to pull out the Rolodex again.

I called George Jenne in Baton Rouge, Louisiana. He'd bought my old station, K102 in El Paso, and he needed a program director. He and Yvonne Guerrero, who would be the GM, met me in Atlanta to solidify the deal. I was hired. It would be about a month before we'd get the station ready to put back on the air. The previous owners had run it into the ground and had taken it off the air completely.

Back in Miami Lakes, now that I had a job, I found myself sitting on a stool at the Last Ditch Attempt Saloon again. I was just about to slip into a blackout when my dealer showed up with the small package of coke I needed to straighten me out.

I don't know why those guys put the cocaine in small little packets folded a dozen times, but this one came that way. As I was unfolding it, it slipped. I tried to catch it, which threw the coke all over the bar top.

I reached over, grabbed a straw, tooted a few hefty lines, and then casually and carefully scooted up the cocaine, putting it back into the little packet and slipping it into my shirt pocket while five or six folks around me couldn't believe their eyes. They were all staring at me when I finally looked up and said, *"What?"*

One of my cohorts at the bar suggested that I go home for a time, leave the cocaine at the house, clean up, change my clothes, and then come back, just in case someone decided to tell on me. I was coming out of the near blackout now, and it made sense. When I got back to the house, which was half a block away, I was able to grasp the seriousness of the situation and vowed to get sober again before I went back to El Paso.

The owner of the station in El Paso that I was about to work for just wanted someone to watch after his property for a while. He hired Yvonne Guerrero and myself to be caretakers more than anything else.

Yvonne had worked as a sales manager at a San Antonio station and was a genuine person. I whimpered back to El Paso, my home away from home, and worked for what now would be known as Power 102. As the program director, I hired John Allen Weitz to be my morning partner.

Also waiting for me was Shirley Skinner, whom I'd met just before going to Miami. She came by the station before we put it back on the air and wanted to go out to dinner, saying that she had split with her husband.

I told her that Mary Ann and I had broken up as well, so we started seeing each other and moved in together shortly thereafter.

I went from B94 FM to Miami and I95, and then to WAIA and back to El Paso in exactly one year, from September to September. What a screwy year. Man, I was lost. The minute I returned to El Paso, I returned to my Alcoholic's Program and my sponsor Ernie. I told him how I had gone back to drinking.

"It's because you don't want to quit," he told me.

"Bullshit, Ernie," I replied. "I want to, but I can't seem to stop."

"You've never taken the first step," he told me. "If you had, you wouldn't be drinking."

"Ernie, I know I'm powerless and unmanageable," I insisted.

"If you absolutely take the first step of Alcoholics Anonymous, you won't drink. You might be a miserable son of a bitch, but you wouldn't drink," he went on.

I told Ernie I wanted to do what it takes to really get sober, once and for all, and he said he'd work with me on it. So began another reasonable period of sobriety as I tried desperately to quit drinking, still without really trying to quit drinking.

By that, I mean that somewhere in the recesses of my alcoholic brain I reserved the right to have one more drink. Not today or next week, but maybe when I take that next trip to Hawaii. I'll drink then and not before.

That's what we call a periodic drinker. So, no matter how much I didn't drink from now 'til that next drunk, I wouldn't get any better as a man. I would not grow. I would be living in the disease, behaving like an alcoholic, and making alcoholic decisions.

It goes back to what the founders of the most successful program of recovery found. It's about *honesty*. Remember the words from The Book about "those who are incapable of being honest with themselves?"

That was I. Sure, not drinking helps in many ways. The bills get paid, you get to keep your job and maybe your spouse, but if you want to grow as a human being, it ain't gonna happen. I had a drunk for a personal consultant.

It's all about being honest with yourself. It doesn't matter how many times you tell others about your good intentions, it's what you believe about *you* inside yourself. All the promises of "never again" and "that was the last time" are a waste of breath if you don't believe them yourself.

Chapter 47
Happy Days

Power 102 went to number one eventually. I was working for a couple of clowns who couldn't care less about anyone, so when I was offered a gig in Milwaukee to work for the Johns brothers, George and Reggie, a couple of Canadian guys who had bought a station there, I jumped on it. George Johns had been phenomenally successful with KVIL in Dallas.

Shirley wanted to go, and ended up working for the station also. I *was* growing weary of myself, and the piece of driftwood that I had become. Sober, clean, and ready to go, we headed off to the frozen tundra of Wisconsin.

I was hired to do mornings for Star 95. I was given a great reception from the people of Milwaukee. We had a fabulous sounding station that played adult contemporary music. For our first promotion, we gave fifty thousand dollars to caller number ninety-five. It was exciting. We burned out our phones lines. Our frequency was, of course, 95.7.

My party didn't last very long, however. For some reason, Reggie Johns didn't favor me that much, so the Johns brothers decided to bring in an old friend, Cat Simon, to do mornings. So, by the spring of 1988, I was looking again. Now, it's not that I was doing a bad job or anything, it's just that Simon had worked for the Johns a couple of times before and they had confidence in him.

Keith Isley, the guy who had brought me in to lead the I95 Morning Zoo in Miami, called and said that he had a new station he was going to run in Miami, and this time wanted me to co-host the morning show and he'd stay. The station was Hot 105.

Chapter 48
Success ... Finally!

J ust ahead of my departure to Florida, I received a homemade, do-it-yourself divorce decree from Mary Ann. It turned out to be legitimate, so I signed it and that was the end of our five-year nightmare. All together, I bet we didn't live together more than one year. Whew! Good riddance.

Within a month or so, I asked Shirley to marry me, and that began a whole new run of pre-packaged insanity with her. It was more like a slow-death approach to Holy Matrimony, but thanks to the longer periods of sobriety, I was able to enjoy longer spurts of a better me.

I95 program director Keith Isley teamed me up with Mindy Frumkes. In Miami, we became known as "Mindy & Malo." Or, "Mindy & The Bad Boy." We were able to take the station to number one in one rating book. Mindy was an extraordinary talent, and a wonderful person to work with and to have as a friend.

Soon, she and I set some record high ratings for Miami. We owned the market for several years. We were still number one when some butt-headed consultant convinced the management of Hot 105 that they should replace Mindy and me with a black guy. Literally, "Guy Black," from New Orleans.

Isley would later tell *The Miami Herald* in an interview that the worst mistake he made in his career was the day he took the consultant's advice to replace Mindy & Malo.

It was a huge mistake. Guy Black came to town and couldn't cut it. Isley asked me if I would come back and do the morning show again. At over six figures, I did, saving every dime I made. Mindy would go back to Power 96, where she had worked before joining up with me. Her gig there lasted several years. I spoke with her the other day, and she sends her love.

Meanwhile, Hot 105 fired Isley, "and here we go, ladies and gentlemen. Where we all go, nobody knows." They also hired Hector Hanibal to be the new program director.

Hector and I didn't get along. He wanted to boss people around, and I wasn't in the mood. When he tried to fire me, the bosses told him, "Oh, no, no, no, Hector. Malo is still the top radio personality in focus groups in Miami." Mindy and I still had the hottest spot on the personality top ten.

I was mostly sober. So now, I was that periodic drinker I mentioned. I have a friend in the program who described herself as a periodic, saying, "Periodically, I wouldn't drink anything for a day or two." It really means that I was able to put some length of time in between each drunk.

One thing all us drunks know is that if you're drinking now and then, or even thinking drinking, you mentally continue to sink deeper into alcoholism. Like I mentioned before, alcoholism is a progressive disease. It never gets better; it only gets worse.

If you suspect that you might be an alcoholic, take the test in the back of this book. Answer the questions honestly, and then take it from there. Don't screw your life up for decades like I did—fix it now. Keep your spouse, your kids, your job, and your life.

I was still working for Hot 105 when the boys from Cox Radio came calling and bought it from E-Z Communications. Oh, boy, Cox Radio again. They were the guys who turned WAIA into The Gator, which, by the way, had to have been the worst possible slogan they could have chosen for the station. Most everyone in Miami is what we call a Gator Hater because of the rivalry between the University of Florida Gators and the Miami Hurricanes.

I didn't care if Cox was buying us. They were a bureaucratic company that didn't do anything without ten people agreeing to it. I was flying out almost every weekend, looking at stations I wanted to buy. The money I earned was terrific, and I had put away just about every dime.

Meanwhile, in December of 1992, when Cox told Hannibal not to fire me because I was still the leader of the list of favorite Miami radio personalities in focus groups, he came to me and got right into my face.

"You better hope you're the top gun on this month's focus list, or you're history," he told me.

I looked at him and thought, "What a waste of time this guy is." As it turns out, I came in at the top again.

"There's going to be six more weeks of winter, at least for you," I told him. Man, he wanted to kick my ass.

Just when I was about to buy a radio station in Victoria, Texas, my old friend John Herklotz made the news. It was Herklotz who had agreed with Roger Christian all those years ago that we should throw all of our attention to San Diego, and take XePRS with Wolfman Jack, et al, down to that fine city, but his partners had overruled him.

Herklotz had just purchased a radio station and a communications site in Santa Fe, New Mexico. I called him to congratulate him, and told him I was looking too. That's when he asked me if I'd be interested in joining up with him as a partner.

It really threw me for a loop, because John was an old friend, one whose word was as good as a contract. He had a great sense of humor, was fun to work with, and offered me total autonomy as the president and GM. I bought forty percent of the corporation, and took great pleasure in telling the wily Hector Hannibal to kiss my ass. I was on my way to Santa Fe.

I would miss Miami. The city and state are electrifying. The days and nights are beautiful, and the lifestyle is cutting edge. There's a golf course on every corner, it seems, and that's where I spent a lot of my time, trying to duck that next drink.

Finally, I had accomplished one of my goals. I had become somebody. I was a big star in Miami, and it felt wonderful. I had spent so many years as a loser. Finally, I had scored one big one on the plus side. I had somehow managed to get my drinking down to about once every six months. I knew that I was screwing with my life, but it was the best I could do at the time.

Chapter 49
The Santa Fe Trail

The radio station in New Mexico was KBOM, or, as we called it, K-BOMB. Our station license was for Los Alamos, where the U.S. government developed the atomic bomb. The "O" in KBOM's logo was a bomb with a fuse coming out of the top of it. The transmitter was halfway between Santa Fe and Albuquerque, New Mexico.

They had rented the south end of a tortilla factory in an industrial park south west of Santa Fe for the studios. New Mexico is an incredibly beautiful place, particularly Santa Fe. The beautiful Sangre de Christo Mountain range is just north of the city. That's where the famous Santa Fe ski basin is located—12,040 feet up. I know that number well, because at the top of the ski basin was where you'd find our communication site. Not our radio station transmitter, but our communications towers, which were a separate division of the company.

When repairs were needed in the winter, our engineers had to take the ski lift up and snowshoe over to the electronics shacks. If it was really bad, we'd have to take the Snow Cat up.

It was a great place for a communications site. When I first got there, the site was generating about $10,000 a month in revenue. When I left, we were billing around $40k per month. It was, as they say, a cash cow. My job was to get that site doing well, so that it could support the radio station project.

KBOM was a mess. We were an oldies station, taking a satellite feed from Westwood One. Steve Scott was doing mornings. Steve was a good guy and a top professional, but I couldn't afford to keep him. I was to be the morning guy, GM, sales manager, part-time engineer, custodian—you name it.

Shirley and I did it all to save dollars and get KBOM earning money. First, I had to stop the bleeding. KBOM was losing about $20,000 per month.

As I was trying to get a grip on what had to be done to accomplish success one afternoon, our bookkeeper for the station said to me, "KBOM is a loser. It will never make money. It will always be a loser."

I couldn't believe my ears. Hey, I'm the new owner—at least humor me a little. I told her, "With that attitude, it doesn't have a chance."

I didn't get on her case too much though, because I didn't want her to quit before Shirley got there to get the books straightened out.

I put together a morning show with Paula Graham, Dave Rarick, and myself. Paula and Dave had grown up in Santa Fe and were local favorites.

The radio ad rates were way out of whack in Santa Fe. One of the problems had always been that the Albuquerque stations could afford better talent and would out-promote the Santa Fe stations. Therefore, the Santa Fe stations were left fighting for scraps and undercutting one other.

I went to every merchant who had ever advertised in Santa Fe and explained that the reason no station could stick it out in Santa Fe was that the rates were just too low to exist.

I promised that, even though I was coming in with higher rates, I would give Santa Fe a local station and the buying audience that comes with it.

It took about six months, but we turned the corner and began to see a profit at that point. We threw a great Christmas party for everyone. Soon, the station would be sold out several days a week. Rates would have to go up. And so it went for several wonderful years.

By the time we sold the station, it and our communication site were valued at about $7 million. We sold KBOM to Russ Withers for $2.4 million.

When I handed the station keys to Russ Withers, I walked away from Santa Fe a happy man. I had finally succeeded. I was rich in so many ways. More importantly, I was finally sober.

Just the year before, on a night on the Big Island of Hawaii, I had been given a preview of the rest of my life. I met a man at the King Kamehameha Hotel that I'd played golf with earlier at the Kona Country Club....

I think this is where we began. I listened to his story and saw my future that night on a bar stool that could have been in any town, anytime, anywhere.

The oddest feeling came over me as the two of us drank that night in Hawaii. I could see he was drifting off into his own blackout world, but as he did, I went in the opposite direction.

I felt so bad for Paul that night, because I knew I was feeling sorry for myself. He was living my future. I didn't want to spend another precious moment on earth drunk. Instead of going into my own blackout, I drank myself sober. I can't explain it. I had enough booze in me to stagger an elephant.

Finally, I just couldn't drink another drop. I felt my own drunkenness leave me. I wanted to give that man the gift of sobriety so badly. I wanted to take that man to a meeting of my Alcoholics, and show him where there was hope. My membership in the program, as tainted as it had been, kicked in, and I never felt more qualified to judge him or myself in my life. Of course, I realized that it was me who wanted these things. I felt so empty right then, because I had failed so many times to get sober. I felt pity for that man, knowing his pain, and knowing the futility of it all, but I was surely also pitying myself for the uselessness of my own life.

As he shook my hand and staggered off to his room, I knew that I had finally had what we in the program call "a spiritual experience." I had a moment of clarity as I stood at the turning point in my life. I wondered if, this time, I would turn in the right direction.

I got down on my knees again that night and asked the Lord to please remove my compulsion to drink. I can't tell you how many times I had asked God to relieve me of the compulsion, but this time, I meant it. This time, I knew that there were no more reservations—no more "one more" times.

It was not because I just didn't want any more trouble. No, this time, I had honestly surrendered; even though my resolve sounded suspiciously like all of the other times, deep in my soul I felt I had finally let go of an old friend—an old friend that almost killed me. It was a definite turning point. Life would be different from this point on.

I was honest with the Lord; more importantly, I was honest with myself, maybe for the very first time. It was a miracle. I went to the Lord asking him to relieve me from the bondage I had imposed upon myself.

"Please, Lord," I pleaded. "Unravel the alcoholic ropes that bind me. Let me know the freedom of life without alcohol, and please, don't let me end up like Paul." This was, as it turned out, the most important prayer of my life.

I was at one of my meetings about three weeks after that trip, when I realized, for the first time in my life, that I had completely lost the compulsion to drink. The Lord had finally granted me the one thing I had kept asking for, but not until I had found the ability to be honest with myself.

I remembered a line from The Book, and I paraphrase: "Some of us suffer from intense mental and emotional problems, but many do recover, if they can be honest with themselves."

No matter how badly I wanted sobriety without being completely honest, I would not have my way, because my way called for "one more drunk"—not today, or next week, but someday, and the Lord knew it. No, the only way was the way it happened.

I wondered to myself if I called the King Kamehameha Hotel and asked if Paul had ever been registered there, would the answer have been, "No?" It had been such a supernatural experience. I felt like one of the Lord's Angels came to me that night and opened the door. I was just glad that I was able to walk through it when given the opportunity.

That was ten years ago. I try to never forget what it was like to live a life of desperation. I don't want to live with shame, lies, and deceit. I don't want to live with sadness, defeat, and feeling worthless. I don't want to ever have to live like that again. I don't want you to live that life either. There is hope; I now live with it.

Even though life still has its ups and downs, the drunk-a-log stopped there in Santa Fe, ten years ago. I haven't had a drink of alcohol, smoked a joint, or in any other way taken a drug for the purpose of getting high since.

Chapter 50
Looking Back

I f I had it to do it all over again, would I change things?

Everything! But would I have the opportunity? Given the same genes and same family environment, I'd probably relive the same nightmare. God only knows why. This life was my destiny.

I love you, Lord, for being so patient with me, and so forgiving.

Shirley and I moved back to my beloved California because I was in constant search for another radio station to buy. Shirley hadn't been willing to take any chances, so for the first year, I just played golf and went to alcoholic program meetings.

Eventually, I wanted something else to do, so I got in touch with one of the local broadcasters here on the central coast of California and they put me to work. Over the next few years, I did a variety of morning shows for them.

Eventually, I was teamed up with Doug Nelson to do news and talk. Doug is a great guy who could have worked in any major market, but he enjoyed his hometown and chose to make his living here. We did a popular show every morning from six to nine. It was three hours of news, and interviews with local personalities and national figures as well. We had lots of fun, and it was a piece of cake.

Chapter 51
Let's Fill That Hole

Just before Valentine's Day a few years back, my wife, Shirley, didn't come home one Friday night. The anguish of knowing that she must have been hurt or killed in an accident on her way home overwhelmed me.

I waited until one in the morning before calling the California Highway Patrol. They said that there were no reported accidents in their jurisdiction, so I gave the police department a call, just knowing that they were going to tell me she had been killed. The dispatcher was a woman, and I could sense that she must have received calls like this before.

She spoke very sweetly to me, as if to say, usually these things don't turn out to be accidents.

"No, we don't have any reports of accidents," she told me. "Why don't you wait a few more hours? She'll probably come home."

That hit me like a ton of bricks. I put that thought on the back burner for a minute, because her path would take her down some dark and lonely streets that cut through a canyon, and then continued on to our house on the beach.

I was frantic as I called the sheriff office and hospitals, but there was no word. I was beginning to think that I might be in denial, but I didn't like the alternatives available. They were all painful.

I was out of my head with worry. I prayed to God as loud as I could to save her life, and I prayed that she hadn't been raped or killed, or both. I told God that I would accept any alternative to her being harmed.

When five am rolled around, I jumped in the shower and just stood, head down, with the hot water rolling off the top of my head. Shirley and I had met like two passing ships in the night back in 1985. We were both in marriages that weren't working.

We had a brief affair before I had to move for my new morning show in Miami. She had told me she loved me, and I had liked that. I thought about her frequently in Miami. I called once and left a message for her back in El Paso, and she saved the note with the message on it as a memento.

Standing there in the shower, I thought of the times we had had together. We'd had some wonderful times together, island hopping around the Caribbean, Hawaii, and in Mexico, not to mention the tremendous success we'd had together in radio. We came out of it millionaires.

I was afraid that she was dead. The water was hot, but my body was shivering down to my bones. I stepped out of the shower. While I was drying off, I heard her voice from the bedroom.

"I'm here," she said, almost in a matter-of-fact tone. "We need to get a divorce," she went on. It was so blunt. I was stunned and couldn't grasp the message she was sending me.

I had been begging for her life, and all she could say was "I'm here, and we need to get a divorce." I asked her where she had been, and she admitted that she had been with another man. I wasn't sure that I heard her right, but I also knew that I had. "What am I living for?" I wondered. I couldn't gather my thoughts.

My brain went on autopilot, and I headed out to play golf like I did every Saturday morning. I knew that if I hadn't, I might have gone off the deep end. Shirley had gained a lot of weight since our marriage in 1988. With the pounds came a snippy, angry attitude that was exasperating. We argued over everything. It wasn't a good marriage.

Finally, Shirley decided to lose the weight and get her life in order. Physically, she did. She went back to being beautiful again, but I was still seeing the "old Shirley," so she went hunting.

It was one of the worst Valentine's Days of my life. Later, my sponsor, Robert, here on the Central Coast, pointed out what a favor the other guy did for me. It lightened my rage a bit, but not completely.

When I met the boys at the golf course, we headed for the first tee. Charlie was the starter and a good friend as well. I thought I might faint.

As we got ready to play, I just blurted out, "Shirley spent last night with some son of a bitch!" Nobody said a word; they were all stunned. Right there in front of all those macho guys, I was as vulnerable as I had ever been in my life. My voice shook. I was afraid that I might break down and wouldn't be able to control my emotions. I just couldn't cry like a baby in front of my friends.

I was determined to hold back as much as possible. It was the first hole on the Oaks course. The tee box is hidden from everything by the oak trees, so we were all alone. My friends came close and gave me support. After a few awkward moments, I stepped up to the tee box. Without saying a word, I ripped the longest, straightest drive I ever hit.

I turned to the boys and said, "That's what I've been missing: a little rage in my game." We all laughed. No one mentioned the affair again that day, but each one of them offered me their love and their homes. Thank God for good friends. Finally, at last, I am somebody—somebody with friends.

Chapter 52
Epilogue

Doug and I continued to do our morning show. I got a condo overlooking the Pacific Ocean and doubled up on my alcoholic meetings. I never felt even a tinge of temptation to drink, but just in case, I wrapped myself up with program friends.

I went to the Humane Society and adopted "Sugar," my little calico kitty cat. When I went to the shelter, they knew me well because I had always made it a point to have them on the air once a week to talk about the pets they had up for adoption.

I was looking for a young kitten, when a year-old calico brushed up against my leg.

"Well, who are you?" I asked as I picked her up. I fell in love with her on the spot.

So, Sugar it was. I took loads of pictures of her in her new home and sent them to the good folks at the Humane Society. The pictures were of her luxuriating on the back of a couch with the Pacific surf rolling in. Ah, the lap of luxury.

She saved my sanity that first year. I looked forward each day to coming home and playing with her and enjoying her little personality. She's by my side as I write these words. Now she's got another calico sister, Sweet Pea, and Fanny Lu and Zoe. I'm a serious cat man. In order to get the last two kitties, I had to marry their mother. It's all about filling that hole.

The Lord wasn't finished with the rewards a man hopes for. Doug and I were asked to host a group of listeners taking them to Hearst Castle in San Simeon for a day's outing.

The day of the event was not the best, unless you like dancing and singing in the rain. There was a torrential downpour. As we got on the bus we had chartered for the event, I noticed that there was an electrifying and handsome woman sitting behind Doug and his wife, Kathy. We welcomed the crowd and drove up to the castle.

I couldn't keep my eyes off her. It was different, though. I felt compelled. It was not some maniacal stare. Rather, I felt directed to her. When we got off the bus, I tried to offer her my umbrella, but alas, she had one of her own.

There was a cute little display of pleasantries between us and I think we both knew that we were being guided to one another, but who knows when it's happening. At one point, it was raining so hard that we put our two umbrellas together and took up a defense against the rain. I felt so cornball when I asked her if she was seeing anybody, but delighted when she said, "No."

We share a love for each other that transcends anything I've ever felt, read, or said. There is no way to describe the feelings we have for one another. We're both crazy about our beloved little felines, and we are both experiencing happiness beyond our wildest imaginations.

There is little doubt in our minds that our marriage was divinely inspired. In my case, standing at the turning point and making the right decision has taken me down the road to happiness.

I told Sandie the other day, "I'm happier than I've ever been in my life." Honestly, I don't think I was ever really happy. Sure, I had happy moments, days, and even weeks, but I was never completely happy, without reservations, until now.

Many thanks for letting me share my story with you. There was a time when I would rather have died than have you hear my story, but now we all know. It's better that way.

If you heard some of your story in this book and want help, or if you know someone who's having a difficult time staying sober, go to my website, www.mynameishoot.com

If you or someone you know has a drinking problem, and you want to do something about it, stay tuned for a few more minutes.

"You must admit you are powerless over alcohol—that your life is unmanageable." Those words make up the first thing you must do in order to get sober.

If you don't do anything else but take this one step, you could stay sober forever. The key to actually taking the step, though, is tricky. It takes honesty. Anyone who has a drinking problem may also be reluctant, consciously or subconsciously, to admit it. Get a sponsor, and don't be afraid to admit your frailties.

Even if you think you're being honest, you may not really be. Deep within your psyche you may be holding out for "one more drunk." That's where the trickiness of the first step comes in: honesty. I couldn't touch it. I didn't understand it. I wanted to interpret it my way.

That's why I lost countless friends, family members, several jobs, and untold opportunities to this dangerous disease. Don't stand in the back of the room when you go to meetings. Listen and share when you have something to say, or if you have a question. Meet people, make friends, and open up your life to other members. Don't be anonymous in the meetings. Get a sponsor immediately.

It's recommended that if you admit to the first step, that you commit yourself to the twelve steps of the rest of the program.

Now, the steps are merely suggestions. My sponsor, Robert, likes to say: "The steps are merely suggestions, kind of like it's suggested that you wear a parachute when you bail out of an airplane."

Don't do things my way and take forty years to get sober. Do it right the first time.

When you realize that you or someone you know may be an alcoholic, know that there is hope. I was hopeless and helpless, with nowhere else to turn, and somehow, I came to be sober, "one day at a time."

Thanks to the Lord and my Alcoholics Program, there is now no doubt that "I am somebody."

God bless you.

Are you an Alcoholic?

Here are the famous twenty questions to help you know the truth.

Ask yourself the following twenty questions, and answer them as honestly as you can:

1. Do you lose time from work due to drinking?
2. Is drinking making your home life unhappy?
3. Do you drink because you are shy with other people?
4. Is drinking affecting your reputation?
5. Have you ever felt remorse after drinking?
6. Have you gotten into financial difficulties as a result of drinking?
7. Do you turn to lower companions and an inferior environment when drinking?
8. Does your drinking make you careless of your family's welfare?
9. Have your ambitions decreased since you began drinking?
10. Do you crave a drink at a definite time daily?
11. Do you want a drink the next morning?
12. Does drinking cause you to have difficulty sleeping?
13. Has your efficiency decreased since you began drinking?
14. Is drinking jeopardizing your job or business?
15. Do you drink to escape from worries or trouble?
16. Do you drink alone?
17. Have you ever had a complete loss of memory as a result of drinking?
18. Has your physician ever treated you for drinking?
19. Do you drink to build up your self-confidence?
20. Have you ever been to a hospital or institution on account of drinking?

If you have answered YES to any one of these questions, there is a definite warning that you may be an alcoholic. If you answered YES to any two, the chances are that you are an alcoholic. If you answered YES to three or more, then you are definitely an alcoholic.

BLOOD ALCOHOL LEVEL MONITORING

The amount of alcohol in your blood stream is referred to as Blood Alcohol Level (BAL). It is recorded in milligrams of alcohol per 100 milliliters of blood, or milligrams percent. For example, a BAL of .10 means that 1/10 of 1 percent (or 1/1000) of your total blood content is alcohol. When you drink alcohol, it goes directly from the stomach into the blood stream. This is why you typically feel the effects of alcohol quite quickly, especially if you haven't eaten in a while.

BAL depends on: 1. The amount of blood (which will increase with weight); and 2. The amount of alcohol you consume over time (the faster you drink, the higher your BAL, as the liver can only handle about a drink per hour—the rest builds up in your blood stream).

Understanding the effects of a rising BAL can be useful in controlling drinking.

Below are the effects of increasing BAL.

.02 A MELLOW FEELING. SLIGHT BODY WARMTH. LESS INHIBITED.

.05 NOTICEABLE RELAXATION. LESS ALERT. LESS SELF-FOCUSED. COORDINATION IMPAIRMENT BEGINS.

.08 DRUNK DRIVING LIMIT. DEFINITE IMPAIRMENT IN COORDINATION AND JUDGMENT.

.10 NOISY. POSSIBLE EMBARRASSING BEHAVIOR. MOOD SWINGS. REDUCTION IN REACTION TIME.

.15 IMPAIRED BALANCE AND MOVEMENT. CLEARLY DRUNK.

.30 MANY LOSE CONSCIOUSNESS.

.40 MOST LOSE CONSCIOUSNESS. SOME DIE.

.50 BREATHING STOPS. MANY DIE.

Provided by the National Council on Alcoholism.

BUY A SHARE OF THE FUTURE IN YOUR COMMUNITY

These certificates make great holiday, graduation and birthday gifts that can be personalized with the recipient's name. The cost of one S.H.A.R.E. or one square foot is $54.17. The personalized certificate is suitable for framing and will state the number of shares purchased and the amount of each share, as well as the recipient's name. The home that you participate in "building" will last for many years and will continue to grow in value.

Here is a sample SHARE certificate:

HABITAT FOR HUMANITY

THIS CERTIFIES THAT

YOUR NAME HERE

HAS INVESTED IN A HOME FOR A DESERVING FAMILY

1985-2005

TWENTY YEARS OF BUILDING FUTURES IN OUR COMMUNITY ONE HOME AT A TIME

1200 SQUARE FOOT HOUSE @ $65,000 = $54.17 PER SQUARE FOOT
This certificate represents a tax deductible donation. It has no cash value.

YES, I WOULD LIKE TO HELP!

I support the work that Habitat for Humanity does and I want to be part of the excitement! As a donor, I will receive periodic updates on your construction activities but, more importantly, I know my gift will help a family in our community realize the dream of homeownership. **I would like to SHARE in your efforts against substandard housing in my community!** *(Please print below)*

PLEASE SEND ME _____ SHARES at $54.17 EACH = $ $_____

In Honor Of: _____

Occasion: (Circle One) HOLIDAY BIRTHDAY ANNIVERSARY

      OTHER: _____

Address of Recipient: _____

Gift From: _____ *Donor Address:* _____

Donor Email: _____

I AM ENCLOSING A CHECK FOR $ $_____ PAYABLE TO HABITAT FOR HUMANITY OR PLEASE CHARGE MY VISA OR MASTERCARD *(CIRCLE ONE)*

Card Number _____ Expiration Date: _____

Name as it appears on Credit Card _____ Charge Amount $ _____

Signature _____

Billing Address _____

Telephone # Day _____ Eve _____

PLEASE NOTE: Your contribution is tax-deductible to the fullest extent allowed by law.
Habitat for Humanity • P.O. Box 1443 • Newport News, VA 23601 • 757-596-5553
www.HelpHabitatforHumanity.org

Printed in the USA
CPSIA information can be obtained
at www.ICGtesting.com
JSHW082155140824
68134JS00014B/246

9 781600 375484